FENG SHUI

FOR LIFE

FENG SHUI FOR LIFE

Mastering the Dynamics between Your Inner World and Outside Environment

JON SANDIFER

Destiny Books
Rochester, Vermont

Destiny Books
One Park Street
Rochester, Vermont 05767
www.InnerTraditions.com

Destiny Books is a division of Inner Traditions International

Library of Congress Cataloging-in-Publication Data

Sandifer, Jon.
    [Feng shui journey]
    Feng shui for life : mastering the dynamics between your inner world and
outside environment / Jon Sandifer.—1st U.S. ed.
          p. cm.
    Originally published: Feng shui journey. London : July Piatkus Ltd., 1999.
    Includes bibliographical references and index.
    ISBN 0-89281-856-5 (alk. paper)
    1. Feng-shui. I. Title.

BF1779.F4 S32 2000
133.3'337—dc21

                                                                          00-043060

Printed and bound in Canada

10 9 8 7 6 5 4 3 2

Dedication

For my sister, Mary, who gave me the gift of a lifetime in 1995 – one of her kidneys – enabling me to continue my journey.

Contents

PART 3
FENG SHUI AND YOUR HEALTH – INNER FENG SHUI 91

PART 4
FENG SHUI AND YOUR HOME 141

PART 5
INTEGRATION 195

ACKNOWLEDGEMENTS

*To all those who have inspired me on my journey of
discovery over the years.*

To my companions in 1967 and 1969 on Kilimanjaro, in 1970 in Spitzbergen and
from 1970–1976 while exploring 52 countries worldwide.

To all the staff, teachers, volunteers, students and clients at the East West Centre
in London from 1977–1994.

To my hosts in all the countries where I have taught: Austria, Belgium, Croatia,
Czech Republic, France, Germany, Holland, Iceland, Ireland, Israel, Italy, Kenya,
Norway, Portugal, South Africa, Spain, Switzerland and the USA.

To the authors who have made Feng Shui more accessible in the West
including: W. K. Chu, Evelyn Lip, Lilian Too, Raymond Lo, W.A. Sherrill,
Man-Ho Kwok, Eva Wong and, of course, their teachers.

To all my friends and colleagues on my own Feng Shui journey who have been
a resource and source of encouragement through their views and insights:
Karen Ayers, Simon Brown, Denny Fairchild, Richard Creightmore, Jan Cisek,
Steven Devine, Bob Sachs, Ron Chin, Stephen Skinner, William Spear, Takashi
Yoshikawa, Gina Lazenby, Karen Kingston, Tony Holdsworth, Kajal Sheth,
Roger Green, Denise Linn and James Moser – thank you all.

Foreword

MY INTEREST IN FENG SHUI first arose in 1976 when, as a Geography lecturer, I came across what I thought was a revelatory approach to the landscape. Chinese Feng Shui experts did not just look at the landscape as an assemblage of rocks and earth, but as something that lives. From this life and energy flowing through the ground they saw very clearly how to build their homes, villages and cities in those places where they would most benefit from this energy, and thus flourish and grow prosperous. For a geographer that was an extraordinary insight, and the fascination of Feng Shui soon took hold of me.

Twenty years later, in the 1990s the focus of attention turned inwards to the interiors of homes and offices and 8 House Feng Shui became popular. Suddenly everyone was orienting the pa kua and checking their best directions. The living energies of Feng Shui were turned towards improving relationships, finding fame and fortune, and enhancing career prospects.

In this book Jon has taken Feng Shui a step further by relating Chinese yin/yang and Five Element theory to you and your journey through life. He takes these first principles and relates them to his own experience in moving from a warm fiery climate to a damp cool one. He relates Feng Shui to divination via the *I Ching* and to the Japanese system of astrology known a 9 Star Ki, and he explains Feng Shui in much more human terms.

By carefully explaining the different schools of thought that come together to create the richness of Feng Shui, Jon helps to disperse some of the difficulties that beginners usually have with this complex subject. At every turn anecdotes from his own experience help to illustrate otherwise complex concepts to the reader.

With the advent of my magazine *Feng Shui for Modern Living* in early 1998 it became true to say that everybody, or at least every woman in the UK, knows roughly what Feng Shui is. The operative word is 'roughly'. Many, pressed to explain Feng Shui, would simply relate the old joke about 'keeping the toilet lid down to prevent the flushing away of chi and wealth', others might say it is an Oriental system for getting what you want, and yet others might explain it as an extension of Chinese astrology. Jon's book helps to fill in the gaps in between these systems and helps to weave Feng Shui, and archetypally Chinese practice, into the context of Western life and culture.

This book also provides hard information and gives simple ways of calculating the relevant 9 Star Ki numbers and how they affect your personal constitution, health and outlook, together with Feng Shui recommendations for improving any deficiencies discovered.

Jon works on what he calls the Inner Feng Shui, which is the balance of yin and yang, to correct the balance of energy in different organs of the body and relates this to our behaviour and health. The careful explanations of how to actually improve your own Feng Shui inside your house or office, is concluded by a real millennium-end updating of Feng Shui by relating it to all sorts of electromagnetic devices, Schumann Resonators, Curry Grids and other electronic phenomena of the last year of the 20th century.

Feng Shui for Life approaches the subject in a unique fashion, and takes you beyond the theory, to reveal how Feng Shui can be of enormous benefit throughout your life's journey.

STEPHEN SKINNER

Introduction

FENG SHUI (which means 'wind and water') is the ancient art of placement. It is an Eastern philosophy that, among other things, determines how you can position and structure the items that make up your personal living space to achieve maximum benefits in terms of health, mental peace, financial success, job satisfaction and spiritual fulfilment. But it was never the intention of the Chinese masters who developed the philosophy of Feng Shui thousands of years ago to suggest that all these wonderful benefits could be achieved by a simple rearrangement of the external trappings of your physical world. Rather, the ancients believed that equal attention should be paid to the inner person in terms of lifestyle factors, such as exercise and diet, channelling the natural energy forces, and working with the powerful influence of the stars. This internalised approach to health is known as 'inner Feng Shui'. Incorporating inner and outer Feng Shui into your daily life may therefore be seen as a journey of enlightenment – and one that also takes in other important spiritual approaches along the way.

My own journey, which eventually led me to Feng Shui, was largely inspired by my upbringing in Kenya. The open spaces, the bustling trading port of Mombasa where I was born, together with the adventures of climbing Kilimanjaro on two occasions in my teenage years, gave me a huge appetite for travel, questioning and exploration. In 1970, as a 17-year-old at school in Britain, I joined three friends for an expedition to Spitzbergen in the Arctic. This became a major turning point in my life and the start of my quest to discover more about the world and myself rather than pursue my academic studies. On my return from the Arctic, I took the equipment from the expedition, a small amount of cash and my passport, and headed off to Dover and began a journey around the world. It lasted some six years and involved travelling through 52 countries, working on ships, down mines, sleeping rough, living with the people of the countries I visited, and throughout this journey, maintaining my health and safety.

It was on this journey in 1972 that I had the good fortune to receive my first real introduction to the opposing yet complementary forces of yin and yang. It came as a gift in the form of a book called the *Tao Te Ching* written by the Chinese philosopher Lao Tzu around 500 BC. It is a very simple yet timeless appraisal of how the dynamics of yin and yang work – socially, morally and cosmically. My very battered *Tao Te Ching* was later joined by my next great discovery – the *I Ching* or *Book of Changes*. This ancient oracle helped me to 'ground' and trust my own intuition as I continued my journey around the world. I finally settled in the UK in 1976 and decided that I would like to study any available systems that were yin/yang based with a view to practising them or teaching them in the future. This led me initially to take up meditation, the Japanese fighting art Aikido and the Japanese system of massage known as Shiatsu. These three systems gave me a practical grounding in my understanding of chi energy, the motivating life force in all things, and I eventually trained as a Shiatsu practitioner and later as a teacher.

Having spent the previous six years travelling and living in predominantly third world countries, I had naturally eaten whatever natural produce was local and available. Now that I was living in the West, however, my diet began to include a high proportion of baked flour products, potatoes, meat, sugar and dairy food. I found this new diet, combined with the cold, damp climate of the UK was having an effect on my chi. A fellow student suggested that I looked into Macrobiotics as it took a yin/yang approach to diet and lifestyle. I took up the system and it was very clear to me that, fundamentally, this was more a philosophy than a diet. Within a few months, I was amazed to discover that I had new levels of stamina, flexibility and vitality that I had not previously experienced. I attended a series of seminars by the Japanese teacher, Michio Kushi, in which he explained the principles of the system and also introduced us to an aspect of Oriental Astrology known as 9-Star Ki. It was all yin/yang based and even had a relationship with the *I Ching* and I immediately felt at home with the system. He also introduced me to the fascinating art of Oriental Diagnosis. I quickly enrolled in his Institute in London to learn all I could about this form of diagnosis and later became a teacher and practitioner. Within a few years, I was directing his Institute in London, designing and co-ordinating the curriculum with other directors in Europe and the USA. Many hundreds of students from all over the world benefited from this unique programme.

Over the years that I taught and counselled individuals about their health and its relationship to lifestyle, exercise and diet, I used the principles of Oriental Diagnosis to understand and assess their condition. The quest was always to discover the underlying cause of any illness. Facial diagnosis, health diagnosis, tongue diagnosis and questioning about diet and lifestyle could provide many of the answers. On other occasions, utilising 9-Star Astrology, I noted from their date of birth that they were currently occupying a 'House' that could lead to certain imbalances in their health. As I broadened my horizons to include areas that were generally beyond the scope of traditional Oriental Diagnosis in assessing a person's condition, I developed an understanding of our relationships, emotional well-being and even destiny from the perspective of 9-Star Astrology. But I still felt there was a link missing. Although I had briefly looked into Feng Shui when I began my studies of Oriental Philosophy in the 1970s, there were very few teachers or books to enable me to take the subject further. In the past 10 years, more and more information has come to light and I now see clearly that this subject was the missing link in my being able to fully understand our own condition and destiny. I now confidently feel that Feng Shui offers the vital starting point for realising our dreams, strengthening our health and grounding our intuition in a very practical way.

When I began as a Feng Shui consultant, I was practising purely what I had learnt from a traditional Feng Shui perspective. Naturally, this was also what the client was looking for. It gradually began to dawn on me that clients were expecting major changes to occur in their life simply by making adjustments to their living space. However, all the years of Oriental Diagnosis training and practice that I continually carry with me enabled me to see things from a wider perspective. First, I noticed that I was only called to the property if there was a problem. Secondly, it was always the client's view that the problem could be resolved simply by adjusting the space. Thirdly, I noticed that although clients were committed to making changes in their external world, they were rarely looking within themselves. Without a doubt, on many occasions there were fundamental Feng Shui flaws within their homes. This could involve glaring examples of a negative energy, such as beams over beds, unstable beds, crystals hung in inappropriate sectors of the home, and evidence of geopathic and electromagnetic stress. While taking a case history, there were occasions when it became apparent that the client had inherited bad predecessor energy from the previous occupants. On other occasions, using my 9-Star Astrology knowledge, it was obvious that they had made a challenging move or that the timing of the move had been really out of line. Wearing my Oriental Diagnosis hat, I noticed that many of the problems the clients had were basically concerned with their physical health, lifestyle, or unresolved issues at work, or with their family or partner.

It has been my privilege to work with many different clients over these past few years and they have largely been the inspiration behind this book. I came to believe that if I could combine the wisdom of Feng Shui with a system of astrology that was practical and easy to understand, and a way of understanding our health (our inner Feng Shui), I could make a profound difference to people's lives. I also wanted to present this information in a way that was accessible, educational and flexible, and which gave everyone the opportunity to shape their own destiny. *Feng Shui for Life* is the result.

I begin by getting to grips with the underlying principles, dynamics and tools that are intertwined with 9-Star Astrology, Oriental Medicine and Feng Shui. All three systems have drawn their inspiration from the *I Ching*, yin and yang and the Five Elements. I then explain 9-Star Astrology which gives a profound insight into who you are, where you are, and which directions to take on your journey. The next section deals primarily with your inner Feng Shui – your health – all drawn from a more modern interpretation of traditional Oriental Medicine. Bringing about changes in your health, and being able to reflect on your condition from time to time, is vital to your journey. It also underpins the most important link within these systems, and that is your own awareness of what is going on. Thirdly, I bring in traditional Feng Shui. In this section of the book I introduce two areas, the first of which, the Form School, is common to all the different approaches to Feng Shui. Secondly, for finer tuning, I use one of the layers of Compass School Feng Shui, known as the 8 Directions system, which is easy to understand and apply to our own lives.

Combining these three areas, I believe, gives you the grounding, the basic skills but most importantly of all, the independence to practise truly effective Feng Shui. After all, who else is responsible for your life, future and destiny?

PART·ONE

PHILOSOPHY AND CONCEPTS OF FENG SHUI

Chapter One

What is Feng Shui?

HISTORY OF FENG SHUI

FENG SHUI IS AS OLD AS THE HILLS — and that is literally where it originated! The earliest known records of Feng Shui originate from the mountainous south-west region of China during the Han Dynasty (200 BC – AD 200). This region gave rise to the development of the predecessor of modern Feng Shui, known as the Form School.

The rugged topography provided the inspiration for a philosophy for finding locations within the landscape that had Sheng Chi or beneficial chi energy, initially for dwellings and burial sites. This energy protected the inhabitants and, in the case of burial sites, allowed the deceased's chi to remain in the 'background' as support for their descendants. This early appreciation that the landscape is a living, breathing entity charged by chi energy provides the backbone to traditional Form School Feng Shui. Chi energy can be potentially distracting and destructive as well as harmonious and energising. With training, experience and intuition, early practitioners could detect where this auspicious chi presented itself and guide those who were not aware of its subtle presence to locate their homes and burial sites.

This perception of the importance of chi energy also underlies early Chinese and even current Chinese thinking about how the body functions. Acupuncture is a fine example of how a skilled practitioner in this field can detect where the chi within a client is blocked or hyperactive and can restore this imbalance through appropriate treatment. Feng Shui and Chinese medicine have another major factor in common.

Prevention is better than cure! Feed, fuel and energise the body appropriately and you will avoid illness and disease. In the same way, locating a home in a well-protected yet energising position will help you avoid problems and difficulties in life.

The Form School was further refined in AD 888 by the teachings and practice of Yang Yun Sung who was, at the time, an adviser to the Emperor. Most scholars accept him as the forefather of a modern interpretation of Feng Shui known as the Compass School. His works are still regarded as classics. Some 100 years later, during the Song Dynasty, they were adapted and further refined by Wang Chih who is now regarded as the main influence on the majority of material studied and practised today that is associated with the Compass School of Feng Shui. This approach to Feng Shui developed on the plains of south-east China where it was naturally difficult to use the principles of Form School Feng Shui, as these were inspired by the mountainous landscape of the south-west.

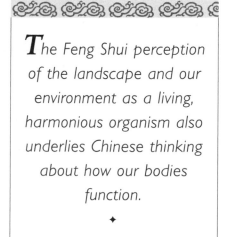

The Feng Shui perception of the landscape and our environment as a living, harmonious organism also underlies Chinese thinking about how our bodies function.

♦

The Compass School incorporates many aspects of the Form School – in fact all modern systems still acknowledge the importance of Form School principles. This means being aware of how chi energy is flowing, not just within the home but also as it approaches. Being able to assess whether chi energy is benefiting or 'attacking' the property is fundamental Form School work. The principle of having what is known as 'support' behind you or your home – as represented by having a mountain behind you – is drawn directly from the Form School. However, the Compass School brings more depth, is more scientific and has evolved in many different directions over the last few centuries. Not all the aspects of the two approaches interface with each other but what they do have in common is a fundamental appreciation of chi and discovering 'where we are' both in time and space.

FENG SHUI TODAY

TRADITIONAL FENG SHUI may have truly been understood by only a few scholars and practitioners. It was principally used by emperors, rulers and military leaders to benefit and protect them in their lives. The lay person had far less access to the science of the Compass School of Feng Shui. Although wealthy merchant families did indeed seek advice from Feng Shui practitioners to help them protect their family, their riches and to enhance their opportunities for success, this complex and fascinating system was not widely understood. Consequently, while respected, and revered by many, Feng Shui was regarded as superstition by others. The huge interest in this subject over the last 10 years has brought Feng Shui on to a new level. For the first time, everyone has the opportunity to understand the basics and to begin to use many of the remedies and complex formulae in their own lives.

There are now several hundred books available on Feng Shui, as well as glossy magazines, journals, societies and associations, schools offering professional training in Feng Shui, websites and shops which supply many of the Feng Shui remedies. Amongst all this information, we have to find our own path through the different styles and approaches to Feng Shui that exist. Essentially, they are all equally valid. All the interpretations by the various schools of Feng Shui aim to bring luck and prosperity to the client or householder. But this can create a dilemma for novices to Feng Shui as they pick their way through the various approaches to decide which they would like to use. Indeed it can cause confusion and even misunderstandings when beginners try to integrate two or three styles, and read about conflicting interpretations of what is essentially the same subject.

Briefly, I will try to summarise from my own experience and research, how some of this confusion has arisen. Firstly, it is important to acknowledge that all this wonderful material originated in China but some aspects of Feng Shui may have had some input from India and Tibet, especially regarding astrology. Next, Feng Shui, like many systems, sciences, arts, philosophies, religions and practices in China, has had to survive numerous revolutions over the past several thousand years. The information that has come down to us today has survived intact. However, it has come to us by different routes. During the 1940s when Chairman Mao took China through the most violent of its many revolutions, a group of inhabitants travelled under the leadership of Chang Kai Shek to find refuge on the island of Taiwan (Formosa). They took with them not only the hope and dream of returning to their homeland but also their cultural heritage. From this island emerged much of the essence and refinement of what is known as 8-House or 8-Mansion Feng Shui.

Hong Kong is another powerful gathering place where a meeting of the particular strengths of East and West created one of the most astounding examples of successful Feng Shui in the world. The combination of the hard-working Chinese people, together with the richness and depth of their practice of Feng Shui, fused in the 19th century with the dynamic qualities of the Scottish colonials who were principally behind the economic development of Hong Kong. This is now where the essence of two astrologically based Compass styles of Feng Shui, The Flying Star and The 4 Pillars, are taught and used extensively.

Malaysia and Singapore, in common with all the other schools of Feng Shui, naturally use basic Form School principles but they also have access to the Flying Star, 4 Pillars and the 8-Mansion from Taiwan. In the West, the main influence in the past two decades has been the work of Professor Lin Yun who introduced his own particular style of Feng Shui to the US, drawn from the Tantric Black Hat sect of Tibetan Buddhism.

Origins of Feng Shui

Developed in CHINA (some influence from India and Tibet)
Form School and Compass School

Hong Kong (former British Colony)

Communist Revolution

Refugees take Feng Shui to Taiwan

Leads to development of Compass Styles

Leads to development of 8 House Feng Shui

Chinese Traders take Feng Shui to Malaysia and Singapore

Undoubtedly, all the different styles and approaches to Feng Shui available at the moment can be confusing. However, personally, I find it very exciting and challenging to work my way through all this material because, underneath it all, the systems revolve around one common factor, and that is yin and yang. I will be discussing this subject further as we continue through the book.

CONTEMPORARY FENG SHUI

THE BIGGEST DILEMMA that most of us face today is how to gain more time. For many, it is an even more valuable commodity than gold! We believe health, wealth, prosperity, luck and good relationships can all be attainable – if only we had more time. This dilemma also faces us when we begin to take a more profound interest in

Feng Shui. To really do the subject justice, we need to read, research, practise, question and then, of course, apply the approach.

Many people have been introduced to Feng Shui through a book, newspaper or magazine article or a television or radio piece. Some have read several books on the subject or have even taken an evening or weekend course. Inspired by a short introduction to this subject, many people go home and do some basic re-arrangement to the layout of their rooms or place a remedy, such as a crystal, in the sector of their home that represents their marriage or wealth. Having done that, I find many people simply wait, hoping for a change. What is often missing in this initial approach to Feng Shui, however, is seeing ourselves from a larger perspective.

I am delighted that Feng Shui and its associated practices are becoming more mainstream in society – it will help so many just to be aware of their space and the basic layout of their home. All of us can benefit from having a home that is free of clutter and that brings in exterior elements such as plant life, water features and more light through the use of crystals, for example. But we also need to appreciate that we help to create our own destiny, our own journey through life. We need to look at our health and current situation and then bring our home into the equation. All of this takes time and, ideally, needs to be simple and practical.

Exploring Feng Shui

✦

- *Read magazines and books*
- *Hire an expert*
- *Fully integrate your health, emotional state and life objectives into the practise of Feng Shui*

Another approach to contemporary Feng Shui is to call in an expert for guidance. This means finding a Feng Shui practitioner through a reputable school or society, or by word of mouth, and getting him or her to visit your home and offer advice. This is an easy way to deal with the issue of time. An expert has many years of experience which he or she can draw on to advise you on the practical steps you can take to enhance your home. The main benefit of this approach is that a practitioner can be far more objective than you in the analysis of your space. Some may take a very scientific or analytical approach to your situation while others may be more intuitive in what they sense, reveal and advise. As with any professional, you would pay for this service and naturally expect a result.

The problem with this approach is that it has the potential to remove you from the equation in actually manifesting the change you are looking for. In my opinion, you are the most vital component in any Feng Shui analysis and ideally are the instigator of any change. You need to be aware of how Feng Shui works and understand the changing nature of the landscape (spatial Feng Shui) together with discovering where you are on your life journey (the astrological aspect of Feng Shui).

FENG SHUI MAGIC

WE DO NOT LIVE IN A perfect world and indeed I believe that life would be boring if we did! Difficulties, challenges, conflicts and even health problems really need to be tackled from a fresh approach if we are to achieve success. Rather than feeling that we are the victim of circumstances and asking somebody else to sort out problems for us, the answer lies in figuring out the cause, establishing our own responsibility for problems and deciding what we can do to bring about change. Some aspects of Feng Shui can be used to protect ourselves, our families, reputation, wealth and even luck. Feng Shui can also be used to stabilise our situation – giving us an even stronger platform from which to move forward. Feng Shui enhances our chances of achieving greater success in our lives. In order to truly benefit from this system, you need to get to grips with the basics, which can often be overlooked in a goal-orientated approach.

As a Feng Shui practitioner and with so many colleagues in this field, it is awe-inspiring to spend time exchanging anecdotal stories where Feng Shui has literally turned round the lives or the fortunes of clients. On a personal level, I would like to share with you an example from my own life where I had initially failed to see the obvious. Several years ago, I decided that I would like to embark on a career in writing as an adjunct to my work as a teacher and a practitioner. I was very clear about the subjects that I would like to write about, what would be involved and how much time it would take up. However, I did not have an agent, I did not have a publisher and I had a modestly filled in-tray of polite refusals from various publishers. I still was not put off and decided to set aside a room – a rather small box room – in my home where I could begin to write and study. I was quite pleased with my efforts, given the space constraints of the room but was completely devastated when a colleague of mine came for lunch one day and had a quick peep into my den. His polite observations left me seeing that I was still a novice and I hastily re-modelled the room over the following 24 hours.

To begin with, I was sitting in a draught of chi – I sat midway between the door and the opposite window – allowing my ideas and inspiration to be distracted. The desk from which I hoped words of wisdom would pour forth was simply a large piece of plywood supported by a couple of trestles! Next, the chair I was using was a rickety, collapsible garden chair with no support at the back and I had stoically been putting up with the discomfort of it! In addition to this, I had my desk facing a blank wall, while in the sector of the room representing fame and reputation was an old black and white photograph of a rally car struggling through the mud that I had driven as a teenager in East Africa, when I had won a competition. Did this image reflect how I wished to be known or was it a true reflection of what inspired me – difficulty/struggle/mud? Piled up behind me on the floor were stacks of notes, books and audio tapes, my valuable study materials that I had accumulated over the years. Shelves to my other side were laden down with more books and more notes.

Within 24 hours I had transformed the space. In came a stable desk, moved away from the wall and with a clear view of the door, a sturdy chair replaced the rickety, collapsible one, and all the notes and books that I did not need were relegated to the attic together with my treasured photograph. By the time I had finished the job, the room had a certain buzz and tingle about it. It felt alive and ready to support any mission that I was on! Over the next few weeks I actually had 100 per cent success in my approach to publishers and ended up with three contracts with three different publishers! At this point I decided I had better quieten down and stabilise the Feng Shui so that I could maintain my commitment and get the job done.

A couple of years later, I thought that it would restore balance in the south-west sector of our living room to introduce a healthy money tree (*Crasula argenta*). Shortly after this, while glancing down the 'for sale' column in our local newspaper looking

Positioning a desk with a wall behind the chair and an inspiring
picture in front of you can lead to positive career developments.

for a second-hand bicycle for one of my six fast-growing children, my eye caught a message in a completely different column. It read 'money plant outgrowing home, buyer collect'.

It seemed like an omen so I called round to have a look at the plant. I was absolutely amazed by this massive money tree which took three of us to move and install in the home. Lovingly cared for by the previous owner, 'Henry' was soon doing his job! Two days later I had the thrilling news that one of my books was going to be published in the USA which is always a British author's dream.

HEAVEN, EARTH, MAN

THE APPROACH I TAKE TO Feng Shui in this book is both practical and tested by my own experience on my journey. From the many years that I have been involved in associated oriental disciplines, I can vouch for their reliability and the profound impact that they can have on our lives. To really benefit most from Feng Shui, it is essential to have a real grounding in the basics. What is chi energy? What are the dynamics of yin and yang and the Five Elements? What is the connection between our inner and our outer worlds? No amount of brilliantly designed Feng Shui is going to have a lasting effect unless you are prepared on many different levels to receive change in a positive way.

Perhaps in your lifetime you have visited a homeopath? You may have been given a remedy which, while being incredibly subtle, could have a profound effect. But what advice will any reputable homeopath give you to go along with the course of treatment? Usually you are told to avoid taking coffee, sugar stimulants, alcohol or any other so-called 'extreme' food that would impede or dull the progress of such subtle vibrational medicine as homeopathic remedy.

The same principles hold true for Feng Shui. The real power of successful Feng Shui lies in:

1. Your involvement

and

2. Setting the stage for change.

The reason I have chosen to integrate a particular system of astrology with aspects of traditional Chinese medicine and spatial Feng Shui is that I see these practices as being interconnected. They represent, in essence, the underlying nature of

Feng Shui is essentially about designing your own future, helping to maximise your health and gaining a true, deep sense of freedom.

◆

Oriental thought. The three lines that make up a trigram, or spiritual symbol, in the *I Ching* express the same idea: man (humanity, ourselves, our health, our destiny) is under the influence of Heaven (our fate, our destiny, our astrology) and under the influence of Earth (our environment, our location, our Feng Shui).

The importance of learning the working principles behind all of these systems is that they give us greater flexibility and a breadth of understanding in all the possible ways of interpreting the material. In all my years in teaching, what I have sought to communicate has been the simplicity of these approaches, making them accessible to a Western mind, adaptable to our current cultural lifestyle and finally, and most importantly, to present the material in a fashion that would not be taken on board by students or clients in a dogmatic way. Having been involved in education these past 20 years, it is probably dogma that concerns me the most. Feng Shui, for me, is essentially about designing our own future, helping to maximise our health and gaining a true, deep sense of freedom. Dogma really does not fit into the equation!

Another observation I have made in recent years is how easy, practicable and accessible Feng Shui can be if approached properly. Some information is far too superficial and really doesn't bring the individual into the equation at all. At the other end of the scale, true traditional Feng Shui with all its calculations and formulae is an amazing skill that, in my opinion, would not only take several years of study to acquire but, more importantly, many, many years of practice. Although it is this traditional approach to Feng Shui that I study and experiment with privately, I would not dream of teaching it, writing about it or sharing it until I had had many years of practice.

The approach I am taking in this book is somewhere between these two poles. I believe that through my seminars, colleagues and friends, I have developed a real feel for what people are seeking in Feng Shui.

I begin with you, by asking you to look at your relationship with the Heavens under the guidance of the 9-Star Ki system of astrology that I have used for over 20 years. Secondly, in setting the context within which you will later apply Feng Shui, I look at health, energy and vitality from the traditional Chinese perspective, but with a more contemporary slant. This is essentially what I call 'inner Feng Shui'. Finally, I bring in spatial Feng Shui – just two layers of it – which is practical, easy to use and yet fundamental to getting on the right track.

We live in a changing world and all of us need some kind of navigational aid that is simple to use to help us on our life journey. The benefit of my Feng Shui approach is that you can do it yourself and do not need to attend lectures or call in the experts. What greater freedom could you have!

Chapter Two

The Journey

T HE STRENGTH — but also the weakness — of our modern society is its desire to analyse and separate out all the components that exist within us and surround us. This has been the drift of modern science over the last 300–400 years. While great discoveries have been made by utilising this approach, it has also meant that we have begun to lose our individual and collective understanding of the interconnectedness of all phenomena. The resurgence in contemporary times of so-called complementary or traditional therapies indicates a desire by many to see beyond this analytical and almost introspective view of ourselves and our environment. For me, our lives, health, history, living space, food, emotions and indeed future, are not simply to be dissected and analysed separately but rather to be experienced. By experiencing all the many factors that form us and affect us, we can gain enormous power to direct our own journey through life.

By only applying Feng Shui remedies without integrating an understanding of our health, needs and astrology, we are only seeing part of the picture. This will also limit the potential depth and power of your Feng Shui practice. Examining our lives and our space through the 'new spectacles' of Feng Shui can reveal the metaphors that surround us in all aspects of our lives. For instance, if you are looking to establish a new relationship or to strengthen an existing one, then of course you can support this by instigating sound Feng Shui principles. However, you could add new dimensions to this process as well. Through understanding your astrological nature, potential and position within the cycles of time you can further support this dream. Add to this improving your health, developing your intuition and, most importantly, focusing your intention, and this will provide added weight and scope for you to achieve what you are seeking. Using the example of relationships, you would therefore need to reflect on where you stand currently. Have you lost connection with your community, family, children or an ex-partner? By beginning to resolve these kinds of issues, you will strengthen your capacity to receive new relationships into your life. A crystal strategically placed in the relationship sector of your home is not enough, in my view!

THE I CHING SYMBOLISM

THE *I CHING* OR ITS TRANSLITERATION, the *Book of Changes*, is widely regarded as probably the oldest book in the world. Written around 3000 BC by the legendary Fu Hsi, the book provides what is basically a code of conduct for people to live by. The book has been used for centuries as a form of divination. It has survived cultural revolutions, where it was either in or out of favour, and it has had commentaries written about it, the most important by the great philosopher Confucius around 500 BC. It could also be regarded as the springboard for Lao Tzu's classic, the *Tao Te Ching*, which was also written around 500 BC and regarded as the origin of what we now call Taoism. The *I Ching's* relationship with Feng Shui is that it provides the foundation of what we could now call yin/yang thinking; the various approaches to Chinese Astrology, divination, meditation, the healing arts and Feng Shui. The value of the *I Ching* for us today is that it can offer us a unique form of guidance when we are faced with difficult decisions in our lives. Used correctly, the *I Ching* can provide profound insights that help us to ground and crystallise our own intuition.

The *I Ching* can help us understand what might be called 'the Order of the Universe'. The book is structured in such a way that it puts into place ourselves, our environment and the influence of the heavens. The manner in which we ask the oracle the questions, how we formulate the responses, and how we interpret its guidance gives us a new direction. In Chapter 3 I will take a closer look at the basic eight trigrams found in the *I Ching* and show how this is not only linked with spatial Feng Shui but also to astrology.

 Essentialy the *I Ching* contains eight different versions of the trigram shown here. The message that these three lines give (whether broken or unbroken) is extremely simple yet quite profound.

THE UPPER LINE

The upper line is used to represent and designate the influence of what we may collectively call 'Heaven'. In whatever culture we hail from, the reference here is to the influence of the universe, planets, heaven, our destiny and even our fate. Its position as the top line of this trigram also implies a movement from above down towards the earth.

THE LOWER LINE

The lower line of the trigram represents the Earth itself, our planet, our home. This line can embody every aspect of our environment – the landscape, the vegetation, the plants, the trees, our food and naturally our own individual dwelling space. The position of this line at the bottom of the trigram also indicates a movement from the Earth towards the heavens.

THE MIDDLE LINE

Sandwiched between these two lines, representing Heaven and Earth, is the middle line of the trigram which represents humanity itself. For the purpose of our own unique Feng Shui journey, this naturally represents us. What kind of astrological influence do we have within our make up being represented in the top line? What kind of home or environment do we live in? Also represented in the lower line is the influence of what we take in from this environment in terms of food, liquid, chi energy and air. Together with these vital components, what are we contributing to our own destiny through our actions and experiences? We have the choice of either resigning ourselves to fate and the seemingly impossible influences of our immediate environment or we can realise where we are and begin to take charge of our own fate.

The Five Ingredients for Successful Feng Shui

INGREDIENT 1: HEAVEN

A VITAL INGREDIENT in all the Compass-based schools of Feng Shui is the component of astrology. There are several different approaches to astrology in Feng Shui and there is much variation over how much importance, relative to our space, is attached to it. Some approaches to Feng Shui would place a far greater emphasis on this side of the equation compared to the actual changes that you could make within the home.

Since Feng Shui is essentially about you and your life, luck and health, it is important to clearly establish 'who you are'. All of us have a unique constitutional make-up from an astrological perspective which can provide important insights into our potential and capacity. Some may regard this as our fate or our destiny. I believe that this can be quite simply de-mystified when we begin to unravel our own unique nature and plot 'where we are' within the cycles of time. In my studies and practice of Shiatsu massage for example, I have always establish 'who' the client was and 'where they were' regarding their astrology. This focused on their areas of vulnerability or success at the time.

I have studied and practised a system of Oriental astrology known as 9-Star Ki – which originates in China. Also known as 9-House or 9-Star astrology, It has been refined, simplified and streamlined by the Japanese in recent years. Almanacs on the subject are available at every railway station in Japan and many take the subject seriously when trying to understand relationships or when planning house moves or a change of job. It is a very practical, simple and flexible system that relates primarily to who you are, your potential and your destiny. There is no direct link in my research to spatial Feng Shui, but it does use the same principles and dynamics, as I will outline in the next chapter.

Knowing which Star rules your constitutional make-up within the nine year cycles that this system uses, can give you a fascinating insight into who you are and your potential. Knowing 'where' your unique Star is as it rotates through the cycle reveals your potential for creativity and change at any given time within the nine years.

Each Star is represented by agricultural imagery, and there are phases within the cycle that represent dormancy, spring, growth, harvesting and so on. Knowing

Understanding your make-up from an astrological perspective, together with knowing where you are on your life-journey, brings a valuable dimension to your use of spatial Feng Shui.

♦

where you are within this cycle of change is vital in planning a successful journey towards your dream.

The third component that 9-Star Ki Astrology reveals is which are the most auspicious directions for us to move in at any given time. This calculation can help you establish a pattern or direction for your journey that helps you work with the tide rather than against it.

Understanding your make up from this astrological perspective, together with knowing where you are on your journey, brings a valuable dimension to your use of spatial Feng Shui.

INGREDIENT 2: EARTH

THIS IS THE MAIN COMPONENT of what we would all consider authentic Feng Shui and concerns our environment. As well as relating to your immediate surroundings, from the broadest perspective it is also important to acknowledge which part of the planet you inhabit.

Beginning with the geography, do you live in the mountains, on the plains, by the ocean or in low marshland? Do you live in an isolated rural location or in a highly concentrated, active, urban environment? The kind of climate that you live in also has an enormous bearing on you and needs to be brought directly into the equation. Do you live in an arid desert climate, a dry mountainous climate, a humid climate or a temperate climate? These seasonal and local variations play a vital role in the appreciation of the Earth's influence upon us all.

All the components necessary for our survival are also drawn directly from this environment: food, water, air and the life-supporting chi energy that the Earth provides. Learning to live in harmony with, rather than fighting against, these vital forces is paramount in incorporating Feng Shui into your life.

For example, you may find yourself living in a dark basement in a damp climate in a cold, lonely, inner city. Dealing with depression and isolation could be high on your agenda. Objectively, you could say that what is missing in this scenario is the influence of the sun – warmth, passion, activity and inspiration. All those factors can be brought into your life by including more of the element Fire. Using practical Feng Shui suggestions about health and lifestyle, there are ways to incorporate this missing element.

If you live in a dark basement flat, striped wallpaper, uplighters and plants such as poinsettias and African violets will bring in uplifting, warm energy.

Finally, the most important part of this Earth environment that you inhabit is your own home. This is where most Feng Shui suggestions are concentrated. It is, after all, the immediate environment that supports you on a day to day, hour by hour basis. By recognising what you feel is missing in your life, you can begin to bring about changes in your home that can act as a stimulus for your needs. By avoiding situations at home where the chi is stagnant or likely to distract you from your journey, you can begin to put into place the basics of Feng Shui. In addition, add to the equation your new knowledge of your astrological make up, your potential and your position on this journey and you can then simply give your dream more stability and direction by instigating changes within your space.

INGREDIENT 3: HUMAN LIFE

AS HUMAN BEINGS we are sandwiched between the influences of both Heaven and Earth. These two factors are pervading our lives at all times and their influence can be subtle, powerful and, at times, confusing. By appreciating the influence that they have on us, we have a greater opportunity to benefit more creatively from our journey. Unaware of these influences, we can often feel a victim of circumstance with little or no control over own own destiny.

> Our lives can become infinitely more manageable and pleasurable if we can firstly understand and take care of our health and, secondly, rid ourselves of the repetitions of previous actions in our lives. Discovering and maintaining good health can, in turn, lead to establishing a firm foundation for our intuition and judgement. With that in place, we are far less likely to get tangled up in the previous patterns that have distracted us from our journey.

I will use the principles of Oriental medicine in Part 3 to help you to establish which aspects of your health you need to work on. What makes this system exciting is that the same underlying principles are used in astrology and spatial Feng Shui. By bringing about changes, for example in your diet, fitness and lifestyle, you are likely to benefit more powerfully from any Feng Shui remedies you choose to use later on. You are simply lining yourself up with your dream so that your Feng Shui practice can focus your intention.

Breaking the pattern of previous cycles of living or behaviour is far more difficult to achieve! Deep down, as human beings, I think we are all a little afraid of change. Although we know it is for the best, change can be a real challenge. If, for example, you are looking for better communication with the outside world, is it enough to know that this is not necessarily your potential as indicated by your astrological make up? Equally, would you blame the missing sector that represents communication in your home or office to be responsible for this 'lack of communication'? From this perspective of Feng Shui, I will be encouraging you to see that all areas of our lives interrelate and that we need to reflect on where we are currently 'out of communication'. Who do you need to be in touch with? Which of those telephone calls do you need to respond to? Have you answered that pile of letters on your desk? Who is that old friend, relative or even neighbour with whom you have avoided any form of contact for the past several years? I believe that until these kinds of issues are resolved there is far less likelihood of your spatial Feng Shui being effective on its own.

INGREDIENT 4: INTUITION

THIS IS A QUALITY THAT is inherent in all of us. We need to acknowledge its existence and use it creatively through constant practice. It is a highly refined sensory capacity and there are times when it works well and times when it seems to fail us! I believe that intuition has a biological basis. When we feel strong, vibrant, energised and clear then our intuition naturally operates in much the same way. However, if we feel tired, despondent, blocked and depressed, then trusting our intuition at that time can often lead to poor judgement and decisions that we later regret. To maximise the potential of creative Feng Shui, we need to be fully in the picture, instigate change and see it through, supported by good health.

One of the best ways to enhance your intuitive capacity is to maintain lengthy but regular contact with the natural world. It is, after all, this environment that fuels and ultimately inspires us. If you feel you are facing a blank wall and seeing no solutions, this is a sign that you need to get out of doors! Contact with the natural elements is vital. A long walk on a windy, even wet day and to feel the rain on your cheeks may not seem like the most re-vitalising pursuit but at least it puts you in touch with two of the Five Elements – Wind and Water. Feel the sunshine on your skin, the power of its rays, even for only a short period of time. Kick off your shoes and feel the earth under your feet or the sand between your toes. Spend time in different types of environments so that each can provide a deep and resonant inspiration. Often, when we are stuck, we are simply attracted to the same kind of vibrational energy and need to force a change.

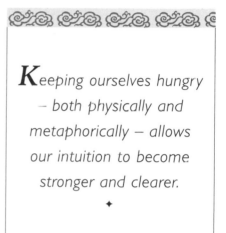

Keeping ourselves hungry – both physically and metaphorically – allows our intuition to become stronger and clearer.

Keeping ourselves hungry – both physically and metaphorically – allows our intuition to become stronger and clearer. If we tend to overeat and lack any challenging exercise, then our biological condition can become stagnant and this is reflected in our intuitive skills. Keeping ourselves 'hungry', metaphorically speaking, is a basic requirement in all traditional oriental studies. In times gone by, this was simply known as developing 'a beginner's mind'. It is not uncommon today to be overloaded with stimuli – be it educational, advertising, the media, and so on. In utilising this approach to Feng Shui, I invite you to keep an open, enquiring mind and to maximise your intuitive capacity by taking care of your health.

There is not much scope for an intuitive perspective in astrology, spatial Feng Shui or even destiny, when it comes to applying classical Compass School Feng

Shui. It is far more of a science and needs to be respected as such. There is a parallel here, I believe, with acupuncture. Acupuncturists do not insert their needles intuitively – they spend many years studying the clinical signs that are taught in Oriental Diagnosis. Their treatment, although it may vary from person to person, is based on a universally accepted methodology. However, my approach to Feng Shui offers you far greater freedom.

INGREDIENT 5: INTENTION

THE FIFTH FACTOR THAT you need to build in to your unique Feng Shui journey is your own intention. This relates to your own will and desire to bring about positive change in your life. This is not about placing a cure in a sector of your home and waiting for something to happen. In the same way, your success with Feng Shui will be limited, even with good professional advice, unless you accept the suggestions you are given.

When you combine the previous four factors of understanding your astrological make up and potential, living environment, current health and level of chi and the clarity of your intuition – you need to complete the picture by bringing clarity and focus to your vision. By declaring both inwardly and externally where you wish to go and what you wish to achieve, the chances of manifesting that change are much greater.

Books, teachers or practitioners of Feng Shui all provide valuable guides to your journey. When I travelled the world, I was always open to suggestions from friends and fellow travellers about places to visit and which route to take. Well-intentioned advice can be of great benefit and save us from making costly mistakes. However, at the end of the day, it is your clear intention that will make real change in your life possible.

As a 14-year-old, I recall struggling up the last 2000 feet of Mount Kilimanjaro in the middle of the night with the encouragement and support of my guide, Obedi. My goal appeared to be a thousand miles away, the angle of ascent looked like 60 degrees and every three steps I took forward, I slipped back one. I gasped for every precious breath as the oxygen at that height was half what I was used to at sea level. In a situation like this, you can be coaxed, encouraged and prodded but unless you have the will to see the situation through, you are unlikely to succeed. Ultimately, I had to make the decision, it was my choice and I chose the easier one, which was to descend!

In Part 4, when we look more closely at spatial Feng Shui, I will again emphasise the importance of intention, particularly when it comes to making adjustments to your own living space. By physically bringing about change within your space, you are giving a solid declaration of your intent that you will be constantly reminded of. Having this intention in mind when you make the adjustments makes it all the more powerful. The images and cures you may use within your home will then simply act as reinforcements and reminders of your intention on this journey.

Chapter Three

The Tools

BEFORE SETTING OUT to discover more about yourself and the fascinating practice of Feng Shui, it is important to familiarise yourself with the underlying concepts that are involved. As you gain practical skill, knowledge and familiarity with these timeless principles, you will begin to realise that they are not only limited to an Oriental perspective on life. Despite more than 20 years of study and practice in this field, I have not become 'Oriental' in my expression, lifestyle or cultural practice. It has actually left me with a deeper appreciation of my own roots, my own culture and how we are all interrelated and intertwined. The 'map' is the same for all of us, it is simply how we choose to interpret it and utilise it that varies.

These dynamic and interactive principles provide the firm foundation for much of the contribution that the Orient has made to the world. This includes traditional Chinese medicine, including acupuncture, moxibustion and herbal medicine, martial arts, meditation, Tai Chi, Qi Kung, astrology, Feng Shui, Oriental Diagnosis, calligraphy, poetry, flower arranging, tactics of war and macrobiotic cookery.

By dipping into these principles, you will have a fuller appreciation of not only the astrology, the health suggestions and Feng Shui remedies that I describe in this book but more importantly, how

The Three Rules of Work

◆

1. Out of clutter, find simplicity

2. From discord, find harmony

3. In the middle of difficulty lies opportunity.

ALBERT EINSTEIN

they interrelate. The beauty and simplicity of all these systems is that they originate from the same stable. Our Western and more analytical approach, however, has tended in the past few decades to separate these various areas and view them as isolated examples of an expression of Oriental thinking. I believe that our potential to find meaningful freedom, happiness and health lies in applying these timeless principles in our lives, rather than in following a rigid set of conclusions drawn from these systems. This ultimately limits the potential for change.

YIN AND YANG

UNDOUBTEDLY, THE PRINCIPLE of chi and yang is the most basic of all those that underpin our practice and understanding of Feng Shui. Yin/yang presents us with the imagery to reveal that our lives, planet, universe and actions are all interwoven. Opposites need to interact if there is to be a spark, movement, dynamism and energy. The early Taoist expression of this polarity is best expressed in the well known diagram shown here.

The yin and yang symbol

In this diagram, the circle represents the unity of all phenomena and the sub division of the shade and the light represents the opposite poles of yin and yang. The small circle of dark within the light and the small circle of light within the dark indicates that within yin there needs to be a little yang and that within yang, there needs to be a little yin. Without this added dimension, we would assume that life was perfectly balanced and neutral. This paradox of the opposites within helps to disprove the idea that everything around us and within us is in perfect harmony and balance at all times. If it was, life would be very boring indeed.

The Chinese scholar Lao Tzu's short but fascinating book the *Tao Te Ching* expressed the dynamism of opposites without actually using the words yin and yang. This classic contains only 81 verses, yet its simplicity reveals the interaction of yin and yang in nature and society at that time. In the second verse he writes 'the hidden and the obvious give birth to each other'. 'Difficult and easy complement each other'. 'Long and short exhibit each other'. 'High and low set measure to each other'. 'Voice and sound harmonise each other'. 'Back and front follow each other'. Later in the book he continues 'we make a vessel from a lump of clay; it is the empty space within the vessel that makes itself useful'. This polarity of opposites continues with his statement 'we make doors and windows for a room; but it is these empty spaces that make the room liveable. Thus, while the tangible has advantages, it is the intangible that makes it useful'.

The complementary yet antagonistic nature of these forces was not only understood in the Orient but is beautifully expressed in one of the recent archaeological finds regarding the teachings of Jesus. In 1945, copies of Coptic writings were discovered in upper Egypt, and scholars agree that they are the writings of an Apostle of Jesus, Didimus Jude Thomas. Unlike modern interpretations of the gospels, these have not been edited and translated over the centuries. Although what Thomas writes has been presented by other Apostles, what is special for me is how close the expression that Jesus uses is to yin and yang. For example, when Jesus is asked by his disciples whether they will enter the 'Kingdom of Heaven', Jesus replied 'when you make the two one and when you make the inner as the outer and the outer as the inner and the above as the below and when you make the male and the female as a single one, so that the male will not be male and the female will not be female, when you make eyes in the place of an eye and the hand in the place of a hand and a foot in the place of a foot, an image in the place of an image, then shall you enter the Kingdom'. In another passage of the gospel of Thomas, Jesus talks of finding the Kingdom of Heaven in a manner that is not unlike the writing of an esoteric Taoist teacher. He says 'the Kingdom of Heaven is within you and it is without you. If you will know yourselves, then you will be known and you will know that you are the sons of the Living Father. But if you do not know yourselves, then you are in poverty and you are poverty.'

In the diagram on page 29, you can begin to see some of the properties of yin and yang. To begin with, high up in Heaven – or infinity – are the origins of yang's nature. Opposite this, emanating from Earth and rising up to return towards Heaven and infinity, is the force of yin.

From a yang perspective, as energy descends from Heaven and brings its influence to bear, the most obvious characteristic of its force is that it creates a downward thrust. As this energy spirals downwards, it begins to concentrate, speeding up in the process and becoming hotter and more highly charged. This concentration of energy inevitably leads to the development of structures that are harder and more concentrated and therefore smaller. This active force of yang brings with it much brighter energy which is symbolic of sunshine, summer and a more active expression.

On the other hand, the force which represents yin's nature originates in the Earth and moves upwards and outwards, returning spirally towards Heaven. Therefore expressions of growth and structures that move upwards, are classified as more yin. As this yin energy rises, it naturally begins to diffuse and slow down and in this

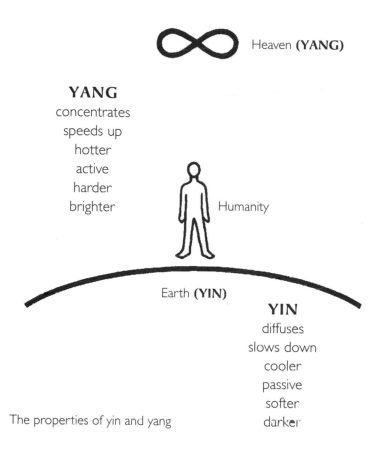

Heaven **(YANG)**

YANG
concentrates
speeds up
hotter
active
harder
brighter

Humanity

Earth **(YIN)**

YIN
diffuses
slows down
cooler
passive
softer
darker

The properties of yin and yang

process, creates structures that are softer and larger. This upwards and outwards growth of energy also allows the temperature to grow cooler. Structures that are softer and movements and activities that are relatively passive are also more yin. Energetically, yin is also associated with stillness, such as the night and the winter, when we recoup our energy. Our behaviour at that time is more introverted, reflective and in many ways, regenerating. From an astrological perspective, the unique 'star' that reflects many aspects of our constitutional make-up may be predominantly more yin or more yang. The yin nature of our star can make us potentially more artistic, intellectual, reflective and service-orientated whereas a more yang star can give us the potential for leadership, focus, tenacity and vocal expression.

As you explore more deeply the astrological aspects of Feng Shui, you will be able to ascertain which 'phase' of the nine-year cycle you currently occupy. Sometimes we are in a more yin aspect – ideal for pursuits that are reflective, contemplative and still, for planning and for taking stock of our lives. Being aware of the more yang phase can benefit us by indicating when to harvest what we have been doing, initiat-

Yin and Yang Activities

✦

YIN
Reading

Listening to music

Gentle gardening

Painting

Tai chi

Yoga

YANG
Swimming

Running

Tennis

Squash

Dancing

Horseriding

ing action or enjoying fame and recognition in our field of work.

As far as understanding health and lifestyle is concerned, you will be able to assess whether your current condition is more yin or more yang – yang being symptomatic of, for example, being restless, impatient, inflexible and hyperactive whereas yin is when we are more tired, forgetful, passive and accepting of situations. Activities and lifestyles that are more 'yangizing' are those which generate heat and make us sweaty or breathless. Exertions which are challenging, physical, competitive and even aggressive fall into this category. Any activity that brings a great deal of focus to bear is also yang. Activities that are more 'yinizing' are those that help us to relax, calm us down, are more intellectual and have a more sensory aspect. In many ways, these are passive, sociable and easygoing pursuits.

Yin and yang also provide the backbone to an initial objective overview of our space from a Feng Shui perspective. Yang living environments would include more concentrated spaces – living in an inner city, occupying a small flat or living and working in a brightly lit environment. A home that uses yang building materials, such as steel, concrete and stone, together with an interior layout that is bright, sharp and modern are all 'yangizing'. The diffuse nature of yin energy would be represented by a rural location, a large spacious home and one that is dimly lit. Building materials that include plenty of wood, and their by-products, or modern plastics have a more yin energy about them. Properties that are old, dark, dusty and especially damp have a high proportion of yin contained within them.

THE FIVE ELEMENTS

AS THE RISING ENERGY OF YIN gives way to the descending qualities of yang, it creates a cyclical process. There are turning points or transformational stages within this cycle which are represented by five specific elements. This concept was first put forward in the early Chinese work, the *Nei Ching* or the *Yellow Emperor's Classic*

of Internal Medicine. This is the earliest known treatise on the background and practice of what we now call traditional Chinese medicine. The interaction and dynamics of this system have not only formed the basis of Chinese medicine but are widely used in the different approaches to Oriental Astrology and in the interior design systems that are born out of Feng Shui.

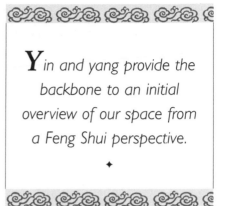

Yin and yang provide the backbone to an initial overview of our space from a Feng Shui perspective.

♦

In astrology, knowing which of the Five Element rules our natal Star gives us a new and fresh perspective on our potential and capacity. Knowing where that star rests each year in terms of one of the Five Elements can give valuable guidance on the kind of activity we could be engaging in. The dynamic interaction of the elements, from an astrological perspective, provide new revealing insights into relationships.

As far as our health is concerned, using Oriental Diagnosis will help you to ascertain which element is currently weak for you. You will then be able to support this through diet, lifestyle and Feng Shui. These adjustments need only be temporary, just long enough to re-balance your health.

From a Feng Shui perspective, the Five Elements are essential factors in supporting your design and implementing any remedies within your living space. When you include the knowledge of 'who you are' astrologically speaking, together with the kind of activity you are engaged in and with the kind of property that you live in, the next issue is which elements will you need to bring in to your life to create balance or to support your dream?

THE DYNAMICS OF THE FIVE ELEMENTS

THE CYCLE SHOWN HERE illustrates very simply the underlying nature of yin and yang that principally drives the Five Elements. The cycle of energy on the left is rising, which represents yin and as it returns to earth and descends on the right, it represents yang. The turning points within this cycle are at the very top and very bottom of this model, and both will tend to have a somewhat similar quality. As the turning points they are changeable and so would be represented by the more plasmic qualities of Fire and Water.

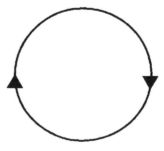

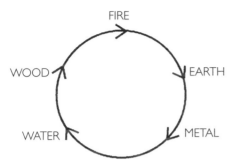

In the diagram here, Fire is graphically expressed as energy which rises while at the same time disperses. Its opposite, Water, is energy that is more still and floats. No two elements in nature could be so completely different, yet they share the common factor of being changeable and difficult to harness. Water is always contained in a bottle, a lake or a glass and Fire needs a home such as boiler or a hearth.

The yin rising energy on the left of the cycle is best represented by the energy of Tree, plant life, new shoots, new beginnings. In traditional texts, this element was known as Wood but I prefer the description of Tree as it embodies the true spirit of initiation, growth and this upward tendency. As the Fire energy on the right subsides, in the natural world it returns to ashes and this is represented on the right hand side of the cycle as the element Soil. This settling, softer, gently gathering energy is rather like compost. In traditional Chinese classics, this element is known as Earth. Soil, for me, represents its supportive, gentle nature. Give this Soil more pressure, more time, more yang and it will consolidate more, focus in on itself and in the process become solid. This phase in the Five Elements is known as Metal and can be best represented by the natural phenomena of rocks and minerals.

Each phase of this Five-Element cycle supports the next one. For example, the rising energy of Tree or Wood is the creator of Fire, while Fire in turn nourishes and forms soil, compost and volcanic ash. Given time and pressure, the element Soil is the creator of, or mother of, the element Metal. Ultimately, under the extreme duress of yang influence, this Metal will metaphorically 'melt', liquefy and this stage is known as Water. In turn, Water is the mother of, the creator of and supporter of the element Tree. This is a vital cycle to understand, both in spatial Feng Shui, Chinese medicine and Oriental astrology.

This nourishing cycle is often known as the mother/child relationship. This concept is vital when you come to interpret and practise the material in the astrology, health and Feng Shui sections of this book. When you find an element that you believe needs to be emphasised, you have the choice of working on the element directly by providing strength, symbolism and support for the element. This means looking for the element that supports the one you are trying to strengthen, and focusing on this element in your remedies.

On a practical level, this could mean that your health may benefit from having more of the Fire element present. You can incorporate the Fire element through the suggestions listed in Chapter 8, while at the same time, bringing in qualities of the

Tree/Wood element to support and nourish the Fire element. The same holds true for relationships in astrology. Again, if you identify yourself as a Fire, then being around others who have the same Fire element gives you a mutual understanding, bonding and support. However, bring a person into your life with the dynamic, supportive nature of the Tree/Wood element and you are increasing your potential for inspiration from that individual. After all, fire consumes wood! In spatial Feng Shui, if you have identified that the

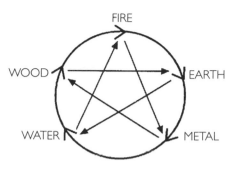

southern sector of your home (Fire sector) needs stimulating, you could bring in elements of Fire to this space such as brighter, fiery colours, candles, or moving objects. Alternatively, you could support this sector with Wood/Tree elements such as plants, light greens or light blues, and uplifting imagery that creates a feeling of youth, energy, movement or dawn.

The second thing to understand about the dynamics of the Five Elements is that they have the potential to override or control one another. This only occurs if one of the elements becomes overcharged, over stimulated or if the element ahead on the cycle becomes excessively weak and does not 'pull its weight'. Here, there is potential for negativity, destruction and immense disharmony.

What I love about this system is that the elements are represented by imagery drawn directly from the natural world which speak powerfully to us. Water out of control will cease to nurture Tree energy but put out Fire. Overactive Fire will ignore the Soil element but melt Metal. Too much Metal and a weak Water element and the Metal will cut across the cycle and attack Wood. This is rather like an axe or a saw being taken to a tree. Uncontrolled pure Wood element will no longer nurture Fire but instead destroy Soil. The imagery here is that wooden implements can dig up soil or that the roots of plants can break up soil or earth. Too much Soil energy will ignore Metal and end up controlling, damming or blocking the flow of Water.

Remember that this potential conflict only occurs when there is either an emptiness or weakness in an element or if the element becomes highly charged and out of control. It is in one of these circumstances that it can have the tendency to ignore its supporting nature for the next element and to cut across the cycle and potentially damage, drain or destroy the opposite element. In Feng Shui, an obvious example of this would be the relationship between excess Water and its effect on the Fire element. Having a Fire sector in your home overloaded with the element Water is naturally destructive towards the Fire element. The Fire sector is the southern aspect of your home or any given room in the house as well. Imagine that this is where your bathroom is, your shower, your toilet, your deep freeze, your refrigerator or where you have chosen to put your auspiciously placed water feature! Not the best solution. From an astrological perspective (explained in detail in Chapter 4), if, for example, a Wood person was provoked and became angry, upset and over stimulated they are most likely to conflict strongly with Soil/Earth people. From a health perspective, the element Fire is associated with the function of the heart. When the heart becomes weak, erratic and out of control, then the immediate concern would be for the function of the lungs controlled by the element Metal which is now in the firing line to receive damage from Fire. In all cases of serious heart disease or failure, the next organ in line is the lungs, and their relationship in acute illnesses is well understood from both the Western and Eastern perspective.

These cycles of control and support can be seen in all aspects of life. When we examine the current state of our collective home – our planet – then using this simple model we can see where we are potentially heading. If we begin by looking at what Soil represents on a global level, we can see it is what we have gathered, what we have stored and the basic resources for our future. Fundamentally, this is our natural environment, our ecology and what reserves we have in terms of potential sustenance for the future. As this element becomes collectively weakened, we can become mistrustful of one another, cynical, despondent and apathetic about the future. This can lead to supporting the negative qualities of all the other elements. The imbalance in Soil supports an imbalance in Metal which can result in collective gloom and negativity. This, in turn, engenders feelings of fear, complacency and inactivity which are the negative attributes of Water. This can then fuel a negative response in our collective Tree energy which is anger, irritability, impatience and violence. Finally, on this cycle, this imbalance of Tree energy will bring out the worst qualities of collective Fire energy which is chaos! This might look a very gloomy picture but there is also a positive side to this cycle.

To counterbalance this negative progress collectively, it would be wise to bring out the best of our Soil nature – compassion. This will engender a feeling of positivity and optimism (Metal nature) which further supports our collective courage (Water). Strong Water nature will bring out the best qualities of our patience, tolerance and flexibility which support the most powerful expression of Fire energy – love. Individually and collectively, the choice is ours.

QUALITIES/CHARACTERISTICS OF THE FIVE ELEMENTS

THE TABLE ON THE next page summarises the characteristics of each of these elements together with their 9 Star number explained in Chapter 4. Here I will outline them in a little more detail.

SOIL

This represents the energy of the afternoon, the late summer and a time of gathering or harvesting. It is a quiet, mellow period. The element Soil or Earth represents compassion, support, richness and is pivotal within the Five Element cycle. The element Soil plays a central role in both spatial Feng Shui and astrology. It governs the function of the spleen, pancreas and the stomach in Chinese medicine, which are all regarded as store houses of the body and the distributors of the harvest. It is the spleen in particular in Chinese medicine that is regarded as our centre, whereas in the West, much emphasis is placed on the importance and function of the heart.

METAL

This represents the energy of the late afternoon and evening when we start to focus in on our homes and families. This is when we leave our work and the fields and gather together. Seasonally, it represents autumn which is the traditional time in a four-season climate for us to gather and store, and complete all our tasks. Metal's nature is about absorbing and assimilating while, at the same time, eliminating what is not needed. In Chinese medicine this is represented by the function of the large intestine and colon.

WATER

This embodies the floating, restful time that is the winter or the night. This peaceful, inactive time has huge, regenerative potential for us all. On one level, it allows for physical rest and mentally it embodies the spirit of self-reflection and meditation. Since 60 per cent of our body is made up of Water, naturally this element controls the function of the kidneys and bladder.

TREE

This embodies the spirit of initiation and dawn. This is an active element which brings newness and freshness to the cycle. It represents spring, youth, vitality, energy, inspiration and enthusiasm. The muscular power and physical stamina is supported by the function of the liver and the gall bladder in traditional Chinese medicine.

FIRE

The upward and outward expression of this element is beautifully represented by the feverish activity that embodies the spirit of midsummer or midday. Nature is in full bloom and full expression. This energy is fully expressed through dance, passion and sharing. This upward, outward, fiery nature fuels the function, in Chinese medicine, of the heart and of the small intestine.

Characteristics of the Five Elements

+ = Positive
- = Negative

Element	Nature	9 Star number	Time	Season	Weather	Organs	Emotions	Behaviour
FIRE	• Upward • Outward • Blossoming	9	Noon	Summer	Hot	• Heart • Small intestine	+ Warm +Passionate - Hysterical	+ Sociable - Erratic - Scattered
EARTH/ SOIL	• Downward • Growing • Earthy	2 5 8	Afternoon	Late Summer	Humid Damp	• Spleen • Pancreas • Stomach	+ Discriminating - Cynical Suspicion	+ Grounded - Poor at completion
METAL	• Inward • Consolida-ting	6 7	Evening	Autumn	Dry	• Lungs • Colon	+ Positive + Enthusiastic - Depressed	+ Clear, direct + Precise - Withdrawn
WATER	• Floating • Dormant	1	Night	Winter	Cold	• Kidney • Bladder • Reproductive System	+ Confident - Fearful	+ Adventurous Flexible - Shy Cautious
TREE/ WOOD	• Upward • Birth	3 4	Dawn	Spring	Windy Changeable	• Liver • Gall Bladder	+ Humorous - Irritable	+ Fun - Rigid

You will be able to refer to the following table as you work your way through this book when assessing your astrology, your health and your spatial Feng Shui. Remember also how these elements can a) support one another b) be supported by a preceding element and c) have the potential to control or be controlled if one particular element gets over zealous!

Examples of the Five Elements

Element	Natal star	Lifestyle	Building shape	Colours	Building materials
FIRE	9	Active Sociable	• Triangular • Spires	Red Purple Mauve Orange	Plastics Glass
SOIL/ EARTH	2 5 8	Grounded Helpful	• Square • Low roof	Yellow Brown	Brick
METAL	6 7	Detailed Serious	• Round • Domes	Silver Grey Gold White	Stone Steel
WATER	1	Reflective Spiritual	• Flowing • Horizontal	Black Dark Blue	Breeze Blocks
WOOD/ TREE	3 4	Active Spontaneous	• Rectangular • Tall	Greens	Timber

THE TRIGRAMS OF THE I CHING

AS WE JOURNEY THROUGH LIFE, we have a choice of either making decisions and choosing directions without seeking counsel or of trusting our intuition. On the other hand, we could choose a route that we trusted, that we understood and that fell in line with our real purpose. 'Going with the flow' is a modern expression of working with the Tao. Literally translated, this means 'The Way'. The Japanese use a slightly different translation which is 'Do'. In both cultures, this means choosing a path in life that we can undertake which will challenge us, strengthen us and ulti-mately give us insights into understanding 'the way'. For example, in the Japanese fighting martial art Kendo – a rigorous yet spiritual approach to fencing – students are encouraged not just to learn the art of self-defence but to discover themselves and their potential through complete mastery of this system. Traditionally, through-out the Far East any discipline that was practised repeatedly was designed to allow the student to understand the Tao.

The *I Ching* – or *Book of Changes* – is probably the most valuable guide any of us can access as we journey through life. Although it is in essence an oracle, when consulted, the wisdom of its guidance can be interpreted on many different levels. Scholars believe that this is one of the earliest attempts by human beings to use hieroglyphics to depict an intuitive understanding of themselves in relation to the greater environment – Heaven and Earth. This was simply presented using eight different versions of trigrams (three horizontally broken or unbroken lines which represented yin and yang) with two of these trigrams combined together to form what is known as a hexogram. This would give the reader of the oracle a potential of 64 combinations. Throughout the centuries, scholars have worked hard to interpret the significance of these combinations as a guide for finding direction when faced with a dilemma. I have listed various editions of the *I Ching* in the Resource Section at the back of this book, which I encourage you to study in more detail.

In spatial Feng Shui and the astrology of Feng Shui, the trigrams and their inter-pretation begin to shape our understanding of 'who we are' (astrologically) and the significance of the different sectors of our home from a spatial Feng Shui perspec-tive. The trigrams are also the foundations of a nine-section grid used in spatial Feng Shui known as the Pa Kua. The trigrams lend their symbolism to each House within the nine-section grid used in astrology which is known as the Lo Shu Magic Square.

As you look at these eight different versions of trigrams, remember that the broken lines represent a yin energy whereas the complete unbroken lines represent the force of yang. Remember also that they are built from the bottom upwards. Simply interpreted, we can look for the strengths and the weaknesses of the trigrams and what they may represent. For example, a trigram may have a yin line at its base representing movement or change. The trigrams also relate to seasons, compass directions, one of the Five Elements, a natural element from the environment and each also represents a particular family member. The eight trigrams shown here relate to the Later Heaven sequence. You will be able to refer back to them from as you study spatial Feng Shui and the astrological system.

CHIEN (the Creative)

TRIGRAM STRUCTURE:	The three yang lines represent the full influence of Heaven and the masculine principle.
FIVE ELEMENTS MEMBER:	Big Metal
FAMILY MEMBER:	Father
NATURAL ELEMENT:	Heaven
COMPASS DIRECTION:	North-west

KUN (the Receptive)

TRIGRAM STRUCTURE:	The three yin lines represent the full influence of Earth and the feminine principle.
FIVE ELEMENTS MEMBER:	Big Earth
FAMILY MEMBER:	Mother
NATURAL ELEMENT:	Earth
COMPASS DIRECTION:	South-west

CHEN (the Arousing)

TRIGRAM STRUCTURE:	The lower line is yang, pushing upwards toward the two yin upper lines representing growth.
FIVE ELEMENTS MEMBER:	Big Wood
FAMILY MEMBER:	Eldest Son
NATURAL ELEMENT:	Thunder
COMPASS DIRECTION:	East

SUN (the Gentle)

TRIGRAM STRUCTURE:	The lower line is yin which is rising toward the two yang lines above, symbolic of growth and penetration.
FIVE ELEMENTS MEMBER:	Small Wood
FAMILY MEMBER:	Eldest Daughter
NATURAL ELEMENT:	Wind
COMPASS DIRECTION:	South-east

KAN (the Abysmal)

TRIGRAM STRUCTURE:	The middle line of this trigram is yang surrounded above and below by yin which represents caution.
FIVE ELEMENT MEMBER:	Water
FAMILY MEMBER:	Middle Son
NATURAL ELEMENT:	Water
COMPASS DIRECTION:	North

LI (the Clinging)

TRIGRAM STRUCTURE:	The yin central line is surrounded and protected by two yang lines. This represents clarity.
FIVE ELEMENT MEMBER:	Fire
FAMILY MEMBER:	Middle Daughter
NATURAL ELEMENT:	Fire
COMPASS DIRECTION:	South

KEN (Stillness)

TRIGRAM STRUCTURE:	The lower lines are yin and are protected from above by yang, suggesting stillness and contemplation.
FIVE ELEMENT MEMBER:	Small Earth
FAMILY MEMBER:	Youngest Son
NATURAL ELEMENT:	Mountain
COMPASS DIRECTION:	North–east

TUI (Joy)

TRIGRAM STRUCTURE:	Two solid yang lines at the beginning give way to the yin line above. The symbolism here is joyfulness and celebration.
FIVE ELEMENT MEMBER:	Small Metal
FAMILY MEMBER:	Youngest Daughter
NATURAL ELEMENT:	Lake
COMPASS DIRECTION:	West

40

CHI ENERGY

THE CONCEPT AND THE appreciation of the existence of chi energy underpins all aspects of Oriental philosophy and life. It is known as Ki in Japanese and the Hindus call this fundamental life force Prana. It is a hard concept for most Westerners to grasp as, since the Industrial Revolution, we have been driven by a more yang perspective of ourselves and our environment. This means that we tend to analyse, dissect and compartmentalise our physical environment and there has been steadily less concern or interest in the vibrational world that exists within and around us. This was certainly not true centuries ago, and the growing interest in vibrational forms of healing – homeopathy, aromatherapy, acupuncture, Reiki and so on are all proof that our fascination in the vibrational world is increasing. As we delve more deeply into ourselves from a scientific perspective, making new discoveries about our chemical, molecular and DNA structure, we will inevitably take that direction to its ultimate conclusion before very long. Naturally, this is a fundamentally yang direction which will open up more inquiry into the yin vibrational world that we co-exist within.

HOW DO WE KNOW IT EXISTS?

Since chi is vibrational, it isn't possible to pin down, categorise or even rationalise. Yet we know that it exists intuitively and indeed practically. Fundamental qualities of chi energy are that it is pervasive and changeable – rather like the concept of Wind and Water that forms the basis of Feng Shui. Our journey through life is indeed changeable, meandering, a series of highs and lows – very much how chi manifests itself. In the English language, and certainly in Western culture, chi could be expressed as our perception of spirit. Practically speaking, this could mean how do you feel? Some days we are happy, vibrant, alert and enthusiastic, while at other times we may feel despondent, stuck, apathetic or uninspired. These are not attributes that we could discover down a microscope but they are very real in terms of our experience, not only of yourself but of the world around us. This is chi energy that we all experience.

The weather that we experience is both pervasive and changeable. The wind, the rain, the gales, the snow, the sunshine and humidity are all expressions of chi and will affect

> *Chi energy is pervasive and changeable – rather like the concept of Wind and Water that forms the basis of Feng Shui.*
>
> ◆

us differently depending upon our condition. After months of gloomy, dark, wet weather in a four seasons climate, we could feel overwhelmed by the glaring sunshine and heat if we were to take a brief midwinter holiday in a warm climate. Conversely, on our return to the damp, wet midwinter from a short, invigorating, sunshine holiday our bodies and our chi will inevitably react to the cold and damp.

Chi energy is also present in the food that we eat. It is not only the ingredients themselves that have different qualities of chi but also how they were prepared and even how they are presented on the plate. Highly processed, packaged, mass produced food may be nutritionally (scientifically) sound but are in their essence lacking in any vitality or chi. Food that is fresh, cooked with love and purpose has strong, vitalising chi whereas food that is re-heated, stale or cooked without any real intention, lacks real clarity and strengthening chi.

We all use our subconscious understanding of chi all the time when we assess one another. When you greet friends or colleagues who you have not seen for some weeks, you are initially noticing their chi. Do they appear happy, sad, tired, lively, friendly, warm, indifferent or distant? We do not assess this information rationally, we are simply picking up on their chi.

THE CHI OF SPACE AND TIME

WHEN WE VIEW POTENTIAL new accommodation objectively, our first impressions are essential. This can never be rationalised scientifically but what we are perceiving and experiencing is the chi energy of the property. Does the space feel uplifting, inspiring, airy or is it gloomy, uninspiring and stagnant? There are no gadgets or meters to assess this. It is simply your perception of chi. Is the chi, the vibration, the legacy of the previous owner still trapped within the walls? Are there sources of stagnant chi close to the property – such as ponds, a cemetery or derelict ground? Are there active, threatening forms of chi which are more yang and are they directed at the property? These could come from busy junctions, railways, tall buildings, telecommunication aerials, etc. Finding sources of any potentially harmful chi like this is part of the process that you will practise later on in the book.

As you delve into the cycles of time that you travel through in life, you will notice that these changing qualities of chi form the rhythms of the cycles. Knowing the kind of chi that is with you and supporting you at each stage of your journey, helps you to plan activities and directions to take that rather than fighting against it. Remember, going with the flow, working with Tao, is what our journey is all about.

This wisdom is within our grasp and by using it wisely, we have the potential to make our journey more effortless and profitable on many levels.

FENG SHUI REMEDIES

Ideally, our living and working environment needs to reflect and support our dream, our vision and our journey. Everything we own or surround ourselves with has its own special charm and potential. Later on in the book, as you begin to have a closer look at your space, it is important to question whether you are carrying excess baggage and whether the things you surround yourself with are a reflection of your journey. Feng Shui remedies, whether they are traditional, authentic or intuitive, all have one major factor in common. They act as a reminder, whether visual, subconscious or symbolic, of the purpose and intention of the journey.

Feng Shui remedies are relatively easy to understand and need to be used wisely with a clear sense of purpose. Simply hanging a finely cut spherical, multi-faceted lead crystal in the window of your office that happens to occupy the sector of your space connected with fame and recognition, may not do its job unless you consider the following:

◆ **Did you place the crystal there with clear intention and focus?**

◆ **Is the window clear and bright to really allow this potential to arrive?**

◆ **Is the area below the window reflecting your receptivity to fame and recognition?**

A crystal that is casually hung in the 'hope' that something might happen and placed in a cracked or dirty window, towering above a dusty filing cabinet full of representations of the 'past' is certainly not going to bring you what you are looking for! Where and when to use these remedies together with the importance of intention will be covered later on.

Feng Shui remedies fall into three categories. These include devices that are protective – these can ward off potentially harmful chi from your home, or devices that are stabilising – designed to keep what is working satisfactorily simmering away or to bring stability where there are potential 'gales' of chi rushing through your home. The final category of remedies are those that we call 'enhancements' – which can uplift or bring greater potential to a sector of your home or can break up chi stagnation within the room or home. Below is a list of common remedies.

PROTECTIVE DEVICES

SHINY/SILVER BALLS – the convex surface nature of a ball combined with a reflective colour helps to ward off or deflect negative chi entering a home via the window. These are usually hung on thread some 15 degrees above your eyeline on the inside of the window frame.

CONVEX MIRRORS – these can be used within the home on landings, passageways and halls to deflect negative chi within the home.

THE PAKUA MIRROR – this is a traditional Feng Shui protective device that is used primarily on the outside of the property to deflect cutting chi if it is threatening the front door – the mouth or gateway to the home. These devices are octagonal in shape, some 4 ins (10 cms) wide and high and have the diagrams of the *I Ching* placed in the Earlier Heavenly Sequence around the outside, and have a central circular mirror which acts as the reflector. These are usually placed above or to the side of the main door.

STABILISING REMEDIES

STATUES/BRONZES – the sheer physical weight and the property of these works of art brings natural stability. The message they convey through their shape and definition has the potential not only to bring stability to space (your environment) but to you in the subtle reminder that they portray.

IMAGERY – photographs, posters, paintings and smaller works of art can provide a continual reminder of stability on a sub-conscious level. A photograph of a mountain represents this far more than a dramatic photograph of two Formula One racing cars on a Grand Prix track!

WIND CHIMES – these are hollow, tubular wind chimes made of bamboo, steel or aluminium that help to break down fast moving chi energy if it is circulating violently through a room, corridor or front door of your home. In certain situations, they can be used to stabilise the heavy downward force of chi that is often a problem on long, straight staircases leading towards a front door.

EARTHENWARE VASES AND BOWLS – the earthy, grounded quality of chi that these artefacts possess can be especially useful for stabilising chi within the home if placed at ground level. Not only are they formed of earth, which has a stabilising quality in the natural world, but also, through their sheer size and weight, they can provide a strong sense of security and stability.

SEA SALT – this has always been regarded as one of the most yang minerals and natural elements on the planet. Their main property is that of preservation. Sea salt can be used to absorb excess yin energy in the atmosphere – whether this is stale chi or simply humidity. Sea salt is used in many space-clearing ceremonies and is favoured by the Sumo wrestlers to dedicate and purify the ring for a bout of wrestling. Old disused salt mines have also been used to store unstable nuclear waste, as its preserving, stable quality is well understood.

ENHANCEMENTS

CRYSTALS – a natural quartz crystal is multi faceted and capable of reflecting the light brilliantly. Hanging one in a sunny sector of your home is going to enhance the vitality of daylight entering your space. Crystals uplift and multiply the quality of light that enters your home and so enhance the quality of your living space at the same time. It is important to make sure that the space you are 'enhancing' is already bright, clear and positive. The size of the crystals also needs to reflect the amount of space you wish to enhance. A big crystal in a small a room can be overbearing whereas a tiny crystal in a massive space will have a negligible effect.

MIRRORS – clean, unflawed, bevelled or framed mirrors double up the space that they reflect. They have the potential to 'open up' a room or a corner that needs to appear bigger in order to reflect whichever aspect or sector of your home you wish to enhance. Mirrors are cleverly used in restaurants to exaggerate the size of the premises and the number of diners present at any time. Like crystals, it is not wise to use them to exaggerate negative aspects of your space.

LIGHTS/CANDLES – any form of lighting is a microcosm of the sun, the most potent life force that we can harness. By using these effectively within our home, we can enhance neglected corners or sectors of our space and strengthen whatever it is we are trying to achieve. For example, candles are excellent for promoting passion, inspiration, reflection and celebration. Strategically placed lights can also be used in this way, especially if they reflect an aspiration of ours on our journey.

IMAGERY – uplifting and inspiring images act both transcendentally and consciously in uplifting our heart, our chi and our soul. If your career, for example, is in the doldrums, then an image representing success or motivation that is placed in the northern sector of your office or home is a subtle daily reminder of your goal. However, a painting that is gloomy or depicts an isolated individual, or a road meandering nowhere all help to increase the sense of despondency around your career or life path.

SOUND – since sound is vibrational energy, it can be used to break up stagnant chi and vitalise space. In traditional times this may have included the use of gongs, wind chimes or bells. A modern interpretation could be your Hi Fi system or your television. They all have a similar effect, to break up stagnant energy and motivate the space vibrationally.

MOBILES – sometimes a room, passageway or part of the garden lacks any movement of chi energy. In this situation, it may be appropriate to use a mobile to help to circulate the chi and thereby prevent stagnation. Mobiles can be brightly coloured or show uplifting imagery. If, in addition, they contain an element of sound, their power is even more effective.

In conclusion, any form of Feng Shui remedy needs to be appropriate, not only to the shape and size of the room and to the effect you are trying to achieve but also needs to suit your taste and personality. If you feel that the best solution in your home would be a wind chime in your hallway, but deep down you dislike them, its effect will be somewhat limited. On a subconscious level, every time you pass the wind chime you are thinking to yourself 'what is that thing doing there' or 'if I hit my head on it one more time, I'll rip it down'. Are these remedies going to attract undue curiosity or ridicule from friends, colleagues and other members of your household? This is where you need to use your intuition and establish what really sits comfortably with you.

PART TWO

FENG SHUI AND YOUR ASTROLOGY

Plotting Your Journey

Chapter Four

Determining Who You Are

FENG SHUI AND ASTROLOGY

IN MY EXPERIENCE, the logical way to approach any form of Feng Shui from a practical perspective is to get 'a fix' on who you are. Any Feng Shui consultant will ask you your date of birth, and perhaps even your place of birth so that he or she can incorporate this vital information into the Feng Shui calculation. Since it is my aim to make this book practical, useful and easily accessible, I have chosen to use 9-Star Astrology as the basis for this section.

I love this system because it is so simple yet, at the same time, so profound. With little skill or practice you can easily get to grips with any situation. Using the calculations that I will explain, you will be able to make new discoveries and also look back at your past life – at your relationships, the moves and decisions you made and judge whether they worked for you or against you at the time.

Starting with your astrological make-up is getting straight to the point as far as Feng Shui is concerned. You are the centre of the Universe, you are a walking Pakua! By working through the astrology section first, and then the health section, you should become well versed in the principles and dynamics that underlie Feng Shui by the time you start to apply it practically.

A vital part of any journey is to be clear about who you are, where you are and which direction to take. Astrology can play an exciting role in this process and I will reveal in this section a system that I have used since 1977. It has provided an excellent means to manifest what I felt intuitively. 'Who you are' means determining your own unique horoscope and I will show you how to calculate this and how to discover your real potential.

The system is based on cycles of nine – be these years, months or days. Knowing 'where you are' within this cycle of time is vital for planning or initiating any activities you have in mind. Choosing the best possible timing gives you far more opportunities for success, rather than simply initiating action and hoping that it will be successful. For major moves in your life you will be able to determine not only when to set out but which directions are lined up auspiciously with your chi energy in any given month or year.

There are many different styles of Oriental astrology which are directly linked to Feng Shui or are connected in some way to the *I Ching*, yin and yang or the Five Elements. Different schools of Feng Shui have their own particular preferences and there is not a great deal of crossover within the different systems. However, they are all grounded in the same philosophy and they are all connected with achieving the same goal which is to determine your destiny. Whether that future is immediate, next year or over your lifetime, all these systems can provide a vital guide. All originate in China and vary in popularity and use according to regional practice.

The best known system is called Tzu Pin or the Four Pillars – and is based on the year, month, day and hour of your birth. A more sophisticated and technically difficult system to master is known as Tzu Wei which has seen a revival in recent years with the advent of computers to help simplify the complex calculations. Another system is known as the 9-House or 9-Star Astrology which utilises the Lo Shu Magic Square to determine the most auspicious directions to face when working and sleeping and also the ideal direction for your front door to face. Again, a nine-year cycle is followed. By knowing the position of your Star as it rotates through this cycle and by nurturing and protecting it as it sits in one of the cardinal or intercardinal directions of the compass you can discover how best to maximise your potential.

I will also be explaining a Japanese system of astrology known as '9-Star Ki'. The expression 'Ki' in Japanese has the same meaning as the Chinese chi. Nine-Star Ki originated in China and evolved from the 9-House system of astrology. Like many other aspect of Japanese culture it was probably brought to Japan by travelling monks.

Nine-Star Ki is very popular in Japan to this day. It is a simple and elegant system that gives us access to a whole new fascinating area. Unlike the Chinese 9-House system, males and females share the same Star and there is no difference in calculation whether you are born in the northern or southern hemisphere. Naturally, with the accuracy of Tzu Pin and Tzu Wei astrology, timing and location of birth is vital in the calculation.

As you begin to understand and practice this system, look at the horoscopes of people in your life, dates of major changes in your past and of major moves you have made. This will help you to develop more skill with this system. For a more in-depth guide to 9-Star Ki Astrology, I recommend my earlier book, *Feng Shui Astrology*.

WORKING OUT YOUR HOROSCOPE

IN THIS SECTION I WILL take you step by step through the process of seeing which three Stars constitute your chart from a 9-Star Ki perspective. The first Star in your chart, which I call your Principal Number, reveals the driving force behind your personality. In a comparison with Western astrology, this would be associated with your Sun sign. The second Star in your horoscope is called your 'Character Number' and reveals the deeper, more hidden side to your nature which is seldom expressed publicly. This Character Number usually emerges when you are under pressure or have your back against the wall. In Western astrology we would call this your Moon sign. The third Star in your horoscope I call your Energetic Number. This shows how you would appear to operate in the world on a more superficial level, how you would go about your daily business and communicate with others. From a Western astrological point of view, this Energetic Number would be associated with what is known as your Ascendant. Put these three Stars together and you can create a profile of yourself which can shed interesting new insights into your character.

One of the greatest discoveries you can make with this system is finding out whether you are utilising the potential you have from the profile you reveal. Too frequently, we are conditioned by parents, mentors and educators into taking a different journey or path in life. Recently, one of the world's greatest authorities on 9-Star Ki, Takashi Yoshikawa, explained his interpretation of the three Stars that make up our horoscope. He compared the first Star with 'what model of car we are', the second Star as showing 'who is driving the car' and finally the third Star expressing 'how we drive the car'. I find those simple metaphors an excellent expression of what 9-Star Ki can reveal about our personality.

HOW TO CALCULATE YOUR PRINCIPAL NUMBER

Whether you are calculating which Star was present in your year of birth or looking to see which Star was present in any year in history, the calculation is the same. In 9-Star Ki astrology, the year usually begins on 4th February and ends on 3rd February the following year. If you are born between 1st January and 3rd February, remember to make your calculation based on the preceding year.

For a quick and easy reference to all the years and stars in question, you can use the chart opposite.

METHOD 1 – for any year within the 20th century you can follow this simple calculation. Begin by removing the 19 from the year in question and then add up the remaining two digits of the year. If the combination of these two digits adds up to a number that is below 10, simply subtract it from 10 and this will give you your Principal Number. **#1**

For example: 1953
= 53
= 5 + 3
= 8
   10 – 8
= 2 Soil Star

If the last two digits add up to 10 or more, simply add them together again until you arrive at a figure that is below 10 and follow the calculation outlined above.

For example: 1946
= 46
= 4 + 6
= 10
   1 + 0
= 1
   10 – 1
= 9 Fire Star

METHOD 2 – the following calculation can be used for any year in history, including the 20th century, 21st century and beyond. Simply add up all the digits of the year in question and keep adding them until you come to a figure of 10 or below. Then simply subtract this remaining figure from 11. This will reveal the Principal Number of the year in question.

Example: 1953
= 1 + 9 + 5 + 3
= 18
   1 + 8
= 9
   11 – 9
= 2 Soil Star

9	8	7	6	5	4	3	2	1
1910	1911	1912	1913	1914	1915	1916	1917	1918
1919	1920	1921	1922	1923	1924	1925	1926	1927
1928	1929	1930	1931	1932	1933	1934	1935	1936
1937	1938	1939	1940	1941	1942	1943	1944	1945
1946	1947	1948	1949	1950	1951	1952	1953	1954
1955	1956	1957	1958	1959	1960	1961	1962	1963
1964	1965	1966	1967	1968	1969	1970	1971	1972
1973	1974	1975	1976	1977	1978	1979	1980	1981
1982	1983	1984	1985	1986	1987	1988	1989	1990
1991	1992	1993	1994	1995	1996	1997	1998	1999
2000	2001	2002	2003	2004	2005	2006	2007	2008
2009	2010	2011	2012	2013	2014	2015	2016	2017

PROFILES OF THE NINE PRINCIPAL STARS

The 1 White Water Star

YEARS:
1918, 1927, 1936, 1945, 1954, 1963, 1972, 1981, 1990, 1999, 2008, 2017, 2026

I CHING SYMBOLISM
Trigram: K'an – Water   **Family member:** Middle Son

PROFILE
The 1 White Water Star will often appear shy and retiring. This deep, brooding nature is part of the profound quality that Water can display. Often philosophical and hiding their strengths, these people think very long and hard before making a commitment or undertaking any major life change. Depending on how the individual is conditioned, they can also appear almost the opposite nature – bubbly, vivacious, attractive and fun loving. The symbolism of Water explains this dichotomy – a deep brooding ocean or a lively mountain stream.

Water, by nature, is adventurous and naturally needs some form of 'container'. Whether it is a glass, bottle or the banks of a river, it needs to know its limits.

The symbolism of the Middle Son means people born under this Star can be great arbitrators and diplomats, both in the family and in a social situation. They can easily arbitrate and help instigate reconciliation. Water, in Chinese medicine, is associated with the function of the kidneys, bladder and reproductive system. Sexually, these individuals can be extremely passionate, but this is not displayed superficially. Many 1 White Water Stars have been successful writers, explorers, philosophers, lawyers and composers.

EXAMPLES
Nelson Mandela, Captain James Cook, Jules Verne, Ken Russell, Antonio Vivaldi and James Joyce.

The 2 Black Soil Star

YEARS:
1926, 1935, 1944, 1953, 1962, 1971, 1980, 1989, 1998, 2007, 2016

I CHING SYMBOLISM
Trigram: K'un – Earth   **Family member:** Mother

PROFILE:
The full make up of yin lines in this trigram represents the strongest expression of female energy – the Mother. These individuals are really at home when they are in a position of service to others. They are bright, energetic and keen to please. They generally fulfil their obligations and get the job done quietly and reliably. They do not necessarily receive the flamboyant recognitions that other Principal Stars might look for. At times they can be fastidious about detail to the point of obsession. They are generally quite conventional, conservative, gentle and tactful.

Their bright, enthusiastic energy needs to be tempered with stability and support in their lives. Their best qualities come forward when they work as part of a family or a team when someone else is making the important decisions and acts as some form of authority.

Whether in the community, family or on the world stage of politics, this star can provide diplomacy and humanity. They make excellent nurses, social workers, personal assistants, bankers or shopkeepers. Any occupation that is service-related supports them well.

EXAMPLES:
Dalai Lama, Tony Blair, Abraham Lincoln, John F. Kennedy, Queen Elizabeth II and Louis Braille.

The 3 Bright Green Tree Star

YEARS:
1916, 1925, 1934, 1943, 1952, 1961, 1970, 1979, 1988, 1997, 2006, 2015

I CHING SYMBOLISM
Trigram : Ch'en – Thunder   **Family member**: Eldest Son

PROFILE:
These are bright, enthusiastic individuals who love the spontaneity of initiating action but are quickly dulled by dealing with detail and the completion of projects. The symbolism of dawn and spring coupled with the energy of the Eldest Son gives them a wonderful spirit of youth. They are very positive people, often high spirited, humorous and talkative. Rather like the eldest son in any family, they are the ground breakers and the ones who have to learn first. As a result, the 3 Tree Star frequently makes mistakes, especially in their youth, but is resilient and flexible enough to bounce back. It is quite common for them to repeat their mistakes or failures but as they approach the age of 27, their path becomes more settled.

They are true pioneers in every sense – breaking the ground for their younger siblings. Many will appear loud and entertaining while, at the same time, having enormous stamina and capacity for hard work. They often excel in sports and make very energetic performers and speakers. Many break new ground by making discoveries in science and art.

EXAMPLES:
Margaret Thatcher, Vincent Van Gogh, Elvis Presley, Mick Jagger, Jim Morrison, Joe Frasier and Sir Frank Whittle.

The 4 Green Tree Star

YEARS:

1915, 1924, 1933, 1942, 1951, 1960, 1969, 1978, 1987, 1996, 2005, 2014, 2023

I CHING SYMBOLISM

Trigram: S'un – Wind   **Family member:** Eldest Daughter

PROFILE:

Where the Bright Green 3 Tree Star represents the yang qualities of dawn, initiation and the spring, the 4 Green Tree Star is a more yin version. They are generally highly intuitive, extremely sensitive and of all the nine stars, probably the most changeable. Like the wind, they have the possibility to be persuaded or influenced by the energy around them or conversely, to be extremely persuasive and influential in their actions. They are usually extremely trusting of friends, family and colleagues around them and sincerely believe that these relationships are inherently good. In forming new relationships, they would always be wise to seek counsel from a close friend or confidante.

People with this Principal Star in their nature have a tendency to 'listen' with their eyes. Some people find this intrusive which others wrongly perceive the intensity of their eye contact to be flirtatious. This is seldom the case. They are simply excellent listeners who match this with unflinching eye contact. Their mood and general direction in life can often change impulsively – rather like the wind and the weather. The trigram S'un begins with a gentle unbroken line leading into the two unyielding lines above. This represents their need for back up and support throughout their lives. They would be wise to avoid situations and conflicts that burn them out. In work, they are ideally suited to planning and mapping out future projects and can work well as travel agents, in transportation and in public relations. Many are also very successful in the fields of broadcasting and film making. Any form of communication suits their gentle yet persuasive nature.

EXAMPLES:

Bob Hoskins, Harrison Ford, Shakespeare, John Logie Baird, T.E. Lawrence (of Arabia), Jimi Hendrix.

The 5 Yellow Star

YEARS:

1914, 1923, 1932, 1941, 1950, 1959, 1968, 1977, 1986, 1995, 2004, 2013, 2022.

I CHING SYMBOLISM

Trigram – none, as they represent the centre of this system.

PROFILE:

The position of the 5 Yellow Star on the spectrum of one to nine is dead centre. Occupying this prominent position puts them at the centre of attention in family and work situations, while at the same time, filling them with a deep desire to be involved in all aspects of family, work and social life. This can often lead them into positions of trust and decision-making. They are not afraid of hard work and although they have a tendency to make mistakes in the early parts of their career, they have the strength and tenacity to try again.

Since they do not have any family representation within the *I Ching*, they can often move into a life of travel and new experiences at an earlier age than most and they will often develop outside of their family. Many with this star as their Principal Number leave home early or become extremely talented and successful at a young age. Coupled with their capacity for hard work and determination, many become successful – particularly in business.

Although the 5 Yellow Star occupies the centre of this system of astrology, it is also the turning point and the beginning and end of a cycle. This brings the possibility of renewal and initiation regarding projects and relationships while at the same time, it can represent decomposition and destruction.

Often naturally sociable, these people can make great diplomats, politicians and the owners of restaurants and nightclubs. Their pragmatic and direct nature can make them unorthodox and ambitious military leaders.

EXAMPLES:

Henry Kissinger, Mahatma Gandhi, Stonewall Jackson, Richard Branson, Henry VIII, Elizabeth Taylor, Greta Garbo, Ludwig van Beethoven.

The 6 White Metal Star

YEARS:

1913, 1922, 1931, 1940, 1949, 1958, 1967, 1976, 1985, 1994, 2003, 2012, 2021.

I CHING SYMBOLISM

Trigram: Ch'ien – Heaven   Family member: Father

PROFILE:

Given that this Star is represented by the *I Ching* symbolism of Heaven and the presence of Father these individuals have an air of natural leadership and authority. They may appear quiet, shy and retiring but they have a very tenacious driving force. They are consistent, prudent and rational in their thinking and actions. The influence of Heaven can make them profoundly spiritual whereas the strong influence of Father can lead them to see the world in a very pragmatic, black and white fashion.

They are frequently extremely direct and honest and are self-critical of their own talents. No one likes to be criticised, but the 6 White Metal Star takes criticism very badly. They frequently lead the way in setting new trends, defining boundaries and in focusing their associates on completing the tasks in hand. Their leadership qualities can appear in all spheres, whether as a director of a company, or the ruler or president of a country, or a moral or military leader. Their grounded, direct, pragmatic nature and sense of justice can make them successful lawyers. Their flair for leadership is often found in the field of sports.

EXAMPLES:

The Duke of Wellington, Napoleon Bonaparte, Pierre Renoir, Pele, Jesse Owens, Sharon Stone, James Dean.

The 7 Red Metal Star

YEARS:
1921, 1930, 1939, 1948, 1957, 1966, 1975, 1984, 1993, 2002, 2011, 2020.

I CHING SYMBOLISM
Trigram: Tui – Lake/Joy   **Family member:** Youngest Daughter

PROFILE:
The trigram for the Lake is comprised of two solid yang lines opening up to the top or surface which is yin so this trigram as has a deep base but a reflective surface. As the youngest member of the family, Youngest Daughter, this Star has learnt from the collective life experience of elder siblings as well as the parents. In life, these individuals have a profound understanding of the ways of the world yet are untroubled by them. It is as if the more responsible parents or elder siblings will take care of the detail and worry.

These individuals are confident, secure, fun loving and sociable. Many enjoy the pleasures of socialising, eating out, entertainment and have a great eye for what is currently fashionable. They frequently appear much younger than their natural age.

They have a very charming nature which expresses itself by their natural talent to listen to others. They make everyone feel at home and at ease. The accumulation of life experience which comes down to them as the youngest child can make them very profound authors or orators. Having the element Metal in their star makes them excellent controllers or advisers in the world of finance. This clarity around Metal supports them well in any job that involves stock control or accounting. Their capacity to listen and to entertain enables them to be counsellors, lecturers, teachers and orators.

EXAMPLES:
George Washington, Georges Jacques Danton, Emile Zola, D. H. Lawrence, Thomas Hardy,, Peter Tchaikovsky, John Keats.

The 8 White Soil Star

YEARS:

1911, 1920, 1929, 1938, 1947, 1956, 1965, 1974, 1983, 1992, 2001, 2010, 2019.

I CHING SYMBOLISM

Trigram: Ken – Mountain   **Family member:** Youngest Son

PROFILE:

The imagery that the Mountain represents is one of stability, strength and stoicism. People with this star as their Principal Number are very hard working and tenacious. Of all the Soil elements within 9-Star Ki – the Mountain is the most yang. If there is a hard or easy way of going about a task, the Number 8 Soil frequently chooses the more difficult route. Often they will repeat mistakes in life yet through sheer dogged determination will inevitably overcome any challenge.

They have a deep sense of justice and their apparently calm exterior is only ruffled when they meet injustice, whether in society, the family or the work place. They love change and revolution but only if it is at their instigation.

Rather like the Youngest Daughter (the 7 Metal Star), these individuals learn from life's experiences. They seldom heed the advice of others and need to discover everything for themselves, even if the process is painful. The result is that everything they know is born out of a real life experience and not one that is intellectual, theoretical or taught.

The reliability and stability of their nature works well for them in any service-related activity, whether as the manager of a company, a shopkeeper, an accountant, farmer or producer. Their great sense of justice supports them well as human rights activists, union officials, lawyers or police officers.

EXAMPLES:

Mao Tse-tung, Yasser Arafat, Lord Horatio Nelson, Charles Dickens, Germaine Greer, Grace Kelly, Johann Goethe, Pope John Paul II, Karl Jung.

The 9 Fire Purple Star

YEARS:
1910, 1919, 1928, 1937, 1946, 1955, 1964, 1973, 1982, 1991, 2000, 2009, 2018.

I CHING SYMBOLISM
Trigram: Li – Fire   Family member: Middle Daughter

PROFILE:
The presence of Fire in the makeup of this star gives the outward appearance of energy, brilliance, flamboyance and even vanity. This bright exterior can often mask a soft, yin interior which could be self-critical, doubting or lacking in confidence. It is important for these individuals to have the acknowledgement, support and recognition of their friends, families and colleagues. Their great strength is their ability to see clearly where others are lost in the fog and to 'shine a light' when others are lost and confused. This bright energy may only come in short bursts but it is profound and motivating to all those around. Many are brilliant at communication and through this medium can inspire confidence and a sense of purpose for those around them. They are passionate, sophisticated and critical, given to outbursts of anger and frustration. Since the energy of Fire must be fuelled, the 9 Fire Star often appears erratic in behaviour and expression. One moment they can be lit up by a new idea and the next moment, they can be either resting or embarking on a new venture. What works for them is emotional support, rest to recharge their batteries and a lot of encouragement from close friends if they go through a phase of self-doubt.

Their open and inspiring nature lends itself well to any job that exposes them to the world. A career in acting, music, politics, public relations, advertising or selling works well for them. Given their great strength in communication, a career in television, radio or customer service is also well suited.

EXAMPLES:
Winston Churchill, Che Guevara, Bill Clinton, William Blake, Monica Seles, Donald Trump, Bill Gates, Mother Theresa, Niccolo Machiavelli.

DETERMINING YOUR CHARACTER STAR

Where your Principal Number relates to the driving force behind you, your true potential in life, your Character Number reveals a more hidden side of your nature. This Star relates to your emotions and can give a deeper insight into how you would react to various situations, particularly under pressure. Only those close to you will know this side of your character and it tends to surface publicly when your back is against the wall.

THE CALCULATION

This is based on both the year and month of your birth. Take a look at the table below and see which one of the three columns your Principal Star occupies on the top line. Now look down the left hand column to find your exact date of birth, and then read across horizontally to the point where the vertical column leads down from your Principal Number. This reveals your Character Star.

Birth Date	1, 4, 7	5, 2, 8	3, 6, 9
Feb 4th – Mar 5th	8	2	5
Mar 6th – Apr 5th	7	1	4
Apr 6th – May 5th	6	9	3
May 6th – Jun 5th	5	8	2
Jun 6th – Jul 7th	4	7	1
Jul 8th – Aug 7th	3	6	9
Aug 8th – Sep 7th	2	5	8
Sep 8th – Oct 8th	1	4	7
Oct 9th – Nov 7th	9	3	6
Nov 8th – Dec 7th	8	2	5
Dec 8th – Jan 5th	7	1	4
Jan 6th – Feb 3rd	6	9	3

For example, if your date of birth is 2nd April 1985, you would begin by establishing that your Principal Number is 6 Metal (5 and 8 = 13, 1 + 3 = 4, 10 – 4 = 6 Metal).

Now look across to where your birth date appears – between 6th March and 5th April. Read across to the final column where the six sits alongside the three and the nine. Simply read down and this reveals that your Character Number is 4.

THE NUMBER 1 CHARACTER

There are two possible natures for the 1 Water Character. Their nature can be cautious, withdrawn, philosophical and deep while other characters can be extrovert, sociable and fun. Generally speaking, however, when under pressure, Water likes to escape – these people will frequently avoid difficult or confronting situations.

THE NUMBER 2 CHARACTER

Deep down, these people are supportive, helpful and diplomatic. They are very tolerant in most situations. Frequently, their unconditional support for others can be abused and they need to protect themselves from being taken advantage of.

Under pressure, this character is looking for a win/win situation. Using all their diplomatic skills and tact, they will want to see conflict resolved with all parties happy.

THE NUMBER 3 CHARACTER

Deep down, these are hard working individuals. They tend to be very expressive, enthusiastic and impulsive. They frequently express themselves freely and openly without thinking through the consequences. However, their warmth and spontaneity soon gets them out of trouble! When under pressure, the trigram that represents 3 Tree (Thunder) will show itself. They can be very explosive.

THE NUMBER 4 CHARACTER

These people have a very gentle and sensitive nature. They are easily affected by the moods and the circumstances of others around them. They are trusting and open and are vulnerable to being drained by other people's unreasonable demands.

Under pressure, rather like the Wind that they represent, they will tend to evade or escape. Rather like Water, with their back against the wall, they will prefer to avoid direct confrontation.

THE NUMBER 5 CHARACTER

In this situation, you will discover that the Principal Star and the Energetic Number have the same element. The 5 Soil character in this respect would simply energise the quality of their Principal Number. The 5 Soil Character can be very self-assertive, controlling and egotistical. They can be bold in whatever they undertake and border on being aggressive when under pressure. Certainly they will hold their ground in any conflict and can ride out most difficulties through sheer dogged determination.

THE NUMBER 6 CHARACTER

Deep down these people will seem reserved by nature. They have enormous inner strength and see and experience the world in a very forthright, logical manner. They are frequently careful and prudent in all their dealings and seldom share what their future plans may be. Under pressure, the full force of Heaven and the authority of Father becomes present. They can be stubborn, immovable and even dogmatic.

THE NUMBER 7 CHARACTER

These people have a deep sense of inner security which gives way to a character which can be playful and independent. They are warm, flexible and sensitive to those around them. Being the Youngest Daughter, there are times when they need to withdraw to brood and reflect.

They will only react strongly if their sense of independence, freedom or self-expression is undermined. It is vitally important for this character to be able to express themselves freely.

THE NUMBER 8 CHARACTER

This character is frequently uncommunicative. A close friend, relative or partner may find them needing their own space while they take stock of their life. Like the Mountain that they represent, they are tenacious and strong. Many can be self-indulgent and this is not wise if they have a tendency to overeat or to gain weight.

Real pressure only exerts itself on the 8 Character when they sense some form of injustice. At this point, they can become extremely explosive, angry and even possibly self-righteous.

THE NUMBER 9 CHARACTER

These people tend to be very warm, passionate and extremely affectionate. At the same time, they like to have these qualities reciprocated in a relationship. They need feedback, they need support. Often bubbly, lively and spontaneous, they can also be rather self-centred and vain.

Under pressure, they will express themselves emotionally in quite a dramatic fashion. Whether this is tears, self-pity, anger or hysteria, it will surface and not be bottled. Once the show is over, they are quick to forget the source of the problem.

DETERMINING YOUR ENERGETIC STAR

THIS THIRD STAR in your horoscope has several interpretations as to its significance. Firstly, it relates predominantly to how you appear to others in your daily life. This could be how you dress, drive your car, cook, communicate and express yourself. Secondly, it is often the 'first impression' that you give the world. A third more profound insight into this star is that, rather like the ascending star in Western astrology, it can relate to your life's challenge. For example, if your Energetic Number was 9 Fire, your challenge in life and indeed what you could work toward improving, would be your communication skills and inspiration to others.

ENERGETIC STAR CALCULATION

You need to refer to the table below which will not only reveal your Energetic Star but indeed your whole horoscope. Begin by looking in the column on the left hand side where the nine Principal Stars are sitting vertically aligned and look across on the top line of the 12 columns to find the precise date and month of your birth. Like

Calculating all 3 Stars

	FEB 4FB-5MR	MAR 6MR-4AP	APR 5AP-4MY	MAY 5MY-5JN	JUN 6JN-6JY	JUL 7JY-6AG	AUG 7AG-7SP	SEP 8SP-7OC	OCT 8OC-6NV	NOV 7NV-6DC	DEC 7DC-4JA	JAN 5JA-3FB
1. WATER	187	178	169	151	142	133	124	115	196	187	178	169
2. SOIL	225	216	297	288	279	261	252	243	234	225	216	297
3. TREE	353	344	335	326	317	398	389	371	362	353	344	335
4. TREE	481	472	463	454	445	436	427	418	499	481	472	463
5. SOIL	528	519	591	582	573	564	555	546	537	528	519	591
6. METAL	656	647	638	629	611	692	683	674	665	656	647	638
7. METAL	784	775	766	757	748	739	721	712	793	784	775	766
8. SOIL	822	813	894	885	876	867	858	849	831	822	813	894
9. FIRE	959	941	932	923	914	995	986	977	968	959	941	932

the years, the months begin slightly later. Rather like in the Character Star calculation in the previous table, you simply line up the columns to reveal all three stars in your make-up.

NUMBER 1 ENERGETIC NUMBER

You could appear indecisive and prone to procrastination. Generally you have a calm manner but given Water's changeable nature, there could be times when you appear erratic as well.

NUMBER 2 ENERGETIC NUMBER

Generally your mode of expression is tactful and helpful. You have a tendency to be fastidious about detail, almost to the point of obsession. You are very good at keeping your word and being on time.

NUMBER 3 ENERGETIC NUMBER

With Thunder ruling this particular star, people around you will find you fairly noisy and expressive. You will appear hardworking, spontaneous and enthusiastic. You are generally much better at having ideas and starting projects rather than completing them.

NUMBER 4 ENERGETIC NUMBER

Most will find you to have a quiet, dependable and gentle nature. You will often go about your tasks in your own fashion and in your own time. You have a pleasing, gentle nature that manifests itself powerfully if you are not put under undue pressure.

NUMBER 5 ENERGETIC NUMBER

You definitely give the impression of being in control. Your presence and appearance can be commanding and even domineering. Without a doubt, your presence will be noticed and felt by all those around you.

NUMBER 6 ENERGETIC NUMBER

You appear very logical and well organised. You always keep your word and are very reliable regarding detail and timekeeping. Your approach to whatever you take on is always pragmatic and straightforward.

NUMBER 7 ENERGETIC NUMBER

Most people will find you very easygoing and laid back in your approach to the tasks in hand. You have an excellent eye and taste for interior design and fashion. You appear charming and have a great sense of humour.

NUMBER 8 ENERGETIC NUMBER

People will find you reserved, quiet or withdrawn. I would describe you as the strong, silent type, always achieving what you set out to accomplish but in your own time and in your own way, even if it is the most difficult or most challenging approach to take.

NUMBER 9 ENERGETIC NUMBER

You will appear impulsive to those around you. Often erratic in how you go about your tasks, you do at least make your presence felt. The 9 Fire will often dress and behave flamboyantly or ostentatiously. Your style and presentation is certainly colourful and on many occasions, full of surprises!

COMPLETING YOUR HOROSCOPE

Now that you are aware of the three major Stars that make up your horoscope, you can place them on the top line of the three columns in the table on page 67. Below that, you could calculate the horoscopes based on the date of birth of various friends, colleagues, family members or your partner, to see how your different stars might relate. This becomes a fascinating process whereby you can gain new insights into your relationships with other people. Why was it, for example, that your younger brother ruled the roost at home? How is it that your colleague at work who is so creative and inspiring often fails to come up with the goods on time as promised?

NAME	PRINCIPAL Star Number	CHARACTER Star Number	ENERGETIC Star Number
Rachel	1	6	9

Chapter Five

Which 'House' Do You Currently Occupy?

YEARLY OVERVIEW

VITAL TO YOUR CREATIVE USE of spatial Feng Shui is knowing all the strengths and the weaknesses of your property. Diagnosing, assessing and implementing changes will be covered in Part 4. However, equally important on your journey is your understanding of your relationship with time. Nine-Star Astrology can provide this potentially exciting and rewarding dimension. As you will see from this system, we all migrate through a nine-yearly cycle and knowing precisely where you are in that cycle can help you plan your journey more effectively and more efficiently.

Now that you understand 'who you are' it is important to find out next 'where you are' on the map. For this next step using 9-Star Ki, it is important only to remember what your Principal Star is. All the 9-Star Ki calculations revolve around cycles of time with nine as the common factor. For example, nine years, nine months, nine days and possibly nine hours, minutes and seconds! The 'map' of this movement of time is the ancient yet elegant model which is known as the Lo Shu Magic Square (see over). It is 'magic' simply because whichever way you add up the numbers of the Square – diagonally, vertically or horizontally – you are left with the number 15.

Each square within this grid is known as a House, and although the Stars migrate around the grid following the pattern in the diagram on page 69, the numbers of each of the Houses are always referred to according to the traditional Lo Shu Magic Square. This means that whatever Star is occupying the top, central House of the Lo

Shu Magic Square at any given time, it is always occupying the 9 House. In the same way, if the 6 Metal Star is occupying the middle left hand House, it is occupying the 3 House.

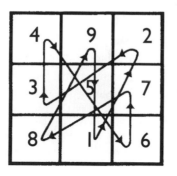

How the Stars move around the Lo Shu Magic Square

This overview of the cycles of change came down to us after centuries of observation by people who were predominantly agricultural. Therefore, the early symbolism associated each House has a seasonal or agricultural flavour. A brief overview of what might lie in store for us as we occupy each of these different Houses could be summarised as follows:

1 Water House – planting, planning, conserving.

2 Soil House – stillness, germination.

3 Tree House – sprouting, spring, initiation.

4 Tree House – rapid growth, blossoming, late spring.

5 Soil House – beginning/end, maturity of growth.

6 Metal House – harvest, prosperity, gathering.

7 Metal House – completion of harvest, celebration, planning for the future.

8 Soil House – stillness, calm before the storm.

9 Fire House – recognition, fame, openness.

In this chapter, I will take you through one aspect of your journey using this form of astrology. By observing which House you occupy in any given year, you will be able to determine what activities or moves are best suited to you at that time. The House that your star occupies in any given year gives the overall flavour of what potentially lies in store for you. It is the general route and direction that you would be wise to embark on that particular year.

It is possible, by using the further calculation in my book *Feng Shui Astrology*, to reveal which House you occupy in any given month. This has a less powerful effect on your chi but it does relate directly to how you feel emotionally and where your strengths and weaknesses may lie in terms of health and communication. A sophisticated almanac, produced annually, can take you to the next stage which allows you to see which House you occupy on any given day. Again, it is less important than the year and the month but it does relate directly to how your chi may be resonating on any particular day you choose to look at; very useful when timing important meetings, presentations or planning short business trips or holidays.

Another analogy you could use to describe these nine-stage cycles would be to imagine that you and I moved in elliptical orbits around the sun. Far away from the sun we would be at our coldest and deeply in our winter (1 Water House), as we approach the sun we would be in our spring (3 and 4 House), leaving the sun we would be in our 6 and 7 House as we become cooler and more isolated, and so on.

HOW THIS BENEFITS YOU ON YOUR JOURNEY

WHETHER YOU DIP YOUR TOE into Oriental philosophy or study it profoundly, the underlying message, whether it is in healing, martial arts or Feng Shui, is to 'go with the flow'. The Tao is the changing world and Universe that we occupy and all these teachings are encouraging us through self-reflection, good judgement and intuition to work with the forces of nature, rather than against them. Nine-Star Ki Astrology is profoundly simple, workable, dynamic and beautiful in the way it portrays the movement of chi energy regarding time. Knowing 'where you are' on the map and taking advantage of the chi that is working with you at any point in time – yearly, monthly or daily – will benefit you on your journey.

I have always used this system to confirm my own intuition. You can use it wisely either to take advantage of the flow of chi in your life at present or to plan or predict the future course that you wish to take on the journey. Either way, it works. As far as knowing where you are in any given year is concerned, use this information wisely as an overview of what potentially lies in store for you. Remember that the symbolism and interpretation has its roots in centuries of simple observation of cycles of change in peoples' lives, the landscape and the seasons. Whether we are living in the 21st century or a medieval society, the principles are just the same. Rulers, strategists and military leaders may have used this wisely thousands of years ago while at the same time, in our own day and age, entrepreneurs, tacticians, spin doctors and public relations strategists have access to the same material which they can use to their benefit.

Another exciting facet of this system can be discovered when you look closer at the people around you on your journey through life. This could be your partner, a colleague at work or a relative.

For example, in the office you may be working alongside someone who has a Principal Star of 3 Tree. Their basic driving force would be their spontaneity, creativity, enthusiasm and stamina for work. However, that is only part of the story. One particular year they may be occupying the 1 Water House, and appear less motivated or withdrawn, very reflective and cautious. You may think there is something wrong with them!

In the same way, you could find yourself occupying the 7 House which is associated with joy, celebration and having fun. Your spouse, on the other hand, may be in the 8 House which has the potential to make him or her uncommunicative and retiring. Rather than thinking something is wrong in the relationship, you can begin to see that it can relate to where the person is within these patterns of nine Houses.

MAKING THE CALCULATION

Step 1 – Remember that all the calculations in this section are based on your Principal Star which, for a quick reference, you can find on page 51.

Step 2 – Decide what year you are looking at. Remember that the year is always from 4th February to 3rd February of the following year. For a quick reference to the principal number for recent and future years, look at the table on page 51.

Step 3 – Now you need to find the Lo Shu Magic Square on page 72 which represents the year in question. This is the square with the number of the year in the centre.

If, for example, you are looking at a 9 Fire year, find the Magic Square with 9 in the centre. Next, see where your own Star sits within this square. Then, see which House your star was occupying in that year according to the according to the Lo Shu Magic Square.

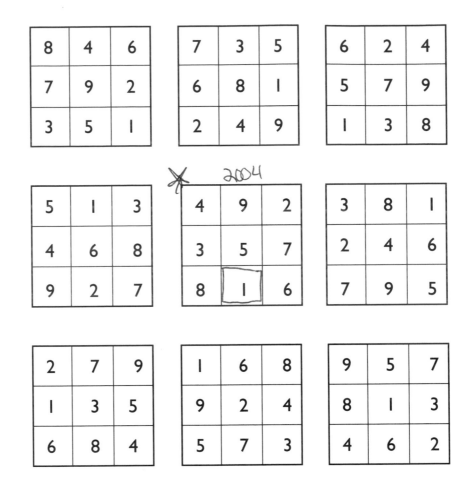

8	4	6
7	9	2
3	5	1

7	3	5
6	8	1
2	4	9

6	2	4
5	7	9
1	3	8

5	1	3
4	6	8
9	2	7

X 2004

4	9	2
3	5	7
8	1	6

3	8	1
2	4	6
7	9	5

2	7	9
1	3	5
6	8	4

1	6	8
9	2	4
5	7	3

9	5	7
8	1	3
4	6	2

Taking an example of the year 2000, which is a 9 Fire year, find the relevant Magic Square above. This is the first square on the top left hand corner . The next step is to see where your star sits within this square relative to the Magic Square. For example, if you are a Number 5 Soil, in a 9 Fire year you would be occupying the 1 Water House. You would then refer to the next section of the book to see what is in store for any star when they occupy the 1 Water House. Simple – if not, read the section again and practise it a couple of times until you get the feel for it. It is not a complicated calculation to make. However, do feel confident that you understand it before moving on to the next stage. It is important that you have grasped these initial calculations before going any further as the next ones are dependent on you understanding these ones!

A good idea at this stage is to look at a year in your life when something exciting or dramatic occurred. Use the previous calculation to figure out which House you were occupying in that particular year. Then you can move into the next section and see what occupying that House had in store for you and check for correspondences.

NAVIGATIONAL HELP FOR THE NINE HOUSES

THE 1 WATER HOUSE

INTERPRETATION

Since the 1 House occupies the north on the Lo Shu Magic Square, this House represents winter, cold and a time for stillness and regeneration. Your vitality and energy this year can be quite low key. Although you are very much alive, this may not appear on the surface. In the same way, if we look out onto a winter's landscape we may assume that it is lifeless – but under the surface bulbs and seeds lie buried, dormant but essentially alive.

LIFESTYLE RECOMMENDATIONS

As this is your winter period and your energy is potentially lower than normal, you are prone to being naturally cautious. This is wise as it is a vulnerable time for you. Be careful about initiating major projects that could cost you dearly in terms of money and vital chi energy. It is a very good time to reflect, to study and to plan your future. In my research, I have discovered many mothers who were pregnant during this particular House.

HEALTH RECOMMENDATIONS

In Chinese medicine, the element Water is associated with nurturing the kidneys, the bladder and the reproductive system. Any inherent weaknesses in any of these systems are quite likely to show up symptomatically while you occupy this House. Kidney energy is particularly vulnerable to the cold and you would be wise to avoid catching a chill, keeping your feet warm and protecting your midriff from cold air. Water energy is also replenished by sleep and it is important to ensure you get sufficient sleep at this time.

Old, unresolved health issues are likely to recur when you occupy this House and may take longer than usual to clear up. This is because the 1 Water House has rather slow, stagnant energy associated with it. If you have a tendency to gain weight, become reclusive or depressive, then you would be wise to make more effort this year to take regular exercise and avoid overeating.

Feng Shui Recommendations

◆

Since the prevailing chi affecting you this year will be coming from the north and is represented by the element Water, place a reminder in your house of the stillness and reflective quality that the Water House brings with it. You could try a still water feature, an image, a painting, a photograph of water, an image of a winter scene, an image that reflects your path or your journey through life.

THE 2 SOIL HOUSE

INTERPRETATION

When you occupy the 2 House, it is important to remember that in the previous year you were in the 1 House which was a fairly dormant year. In the 2 House your energy begins to pick up and although you are still feeling the effects of the winter, you will undoubtedly begin to see a light at the end of the tunnel. It is generally not a dramatic House to occupy with few major ups and downs. Rather like the 1 Water House, you could easily find yourself being unusually quiet, reserved, conservative, cautious and even pessimistic.

LIFESTYLE RECOMMENDATIONS

Next year you will be moving into the 3 House which represents spring. While you are still in the 2 House it would be wise to begin to prepare yourself for utilising this forthcoming energy and enthusiasm. Perhaps the ideas and schemes that have occupied you in the 1 House can begin to shape up on a planning level. It is a perfect time to explore possibilities with new partners, make enquiries about loans and courses and begin to chart the future of some new enterprise that you would like to undertake.

If you are a parent or someone in a position of authority at work, it is a time to listen rather than to take a commanding role. This should not lessen your involvement in key decision-making processes, but do take more time to listen to those around you.

HEALTH RECOMMENDATIONS

The energy of Soil or Earth in Chinese medicine is associated with recharging the spleen, the pancreas and the stomach. All three of these organs are more vulnerable to any form of refined carbohydrate, especially cakes, white bread, biscuits and of course, sugar. Be moderate in your intake and make sure that you take plenty of exercise as the 2 House is still a relatively stagnant House on all levels.

Feng Shui Recommendations

♦

In the south-west sector of a room or your home activate the chi, which begins to rise when you occupy the 2 House, with a mild element of Fire. I strongly recommend an uplighter in this sector. Since this House also represents relatively still chi – an awakening from the winter – any remedy needs to be soft rather than too brazen. The Soil/Earth Element of this sector could be activated by a crystal, for example.

THE 3 TREE HOUSE

INTERPRETATION

Here, the relative stagnation of the previous two years (1 House and 2 House) recedes and you will feel the effect of this new found Tree energy in your life. The 3 House is associated with the dawn, the spring, new growth, initiation and re-invention. It can be a particularly inspiring House to occupy. The schemes and dreams of the past two years can begin to grow and flourish while at the same time whatever you have been involved in will start to grow. This could mean that carefully planned new ventures will take off while unresolved emotional, financial or health issues could spiral out of control.

LIFESTYLE RECOMMENDATIONS

With the full force of spring backing your chi energy this year, whatever you initiate or begin to undertake will move at considerable speed. It is therefore essential that you remain clear about where you want to go and what you want to do in your life. Whatever you initiate or undertake this year, it is likely to have a fairly long-term effect.

Try to avoid situations or people who slow you down with their lack of enthusiasm or pessimism. It is important to get behind the momentum and to make sure that it is all heading in a positive direction that will benefit you and those around you.

HEALTH RECOMMENDATIONS
Tree or Wood energy in Chinese medicine is the support behind the function of the liver and the gall-bladder. Both these organs can make us flexible, adaptable and humorous. Plenty of appropriate physical exercise is important for you this year. Getting up early to catch the energy of dawn is essential. Avoid eating late at night as this stagnates the liver and gall-bladder. Try to reduce foods that the liver and gall-bladder have to work hard to assimilate such as fatty foods, raw oil and well cooked dairy products. Bring a little sharpness onto your plate with condiments such as spring onions, good quality vinegar, lemon juice or sharp-tasting pickles.

Feng Shui Recommendations

✦

Your chi is being charged more strongly in the eastern sector of your home – which is characterised by the Wood/Tree element. Activate this sector with either an uplighter, a healthy, vibrant plant or a bubbling water feature. Any imagery or reminder of what you are trying to initiate at present would also be beneficial.

THE 4 TREE HOUSE

INTERPRETATION
This year you find yourself occupying a House that builds on the momentum and growth of the previous year. All the growth and activity is now charging ahead – you are unstoppable! If all is going well, you are likely to feel very positive and almost overwhelmed by the sheer pleasure and success of what you are doing. If, however, you are not very centred, then you are likely to feel unnerved, rattled and almost out of control.

LIFESTYLE RECOMMENDATIONS
Since you are feeling the full momentum of whatever it is you have been planning, building and developing, it is very unwise for you to change course in a dramatic

fashion this particular year. By all means change your job but stay within the same field. It is rather like a farmer who has planted pumpkin seeds, nurtured them, fertilised them and then decides just prior to the harvest that he is going to give up growing pumpkins and start to cultivate parsnips! Stay focused.

Your new-found enthusiasm will often let you get carried away. Be very careful not to over commit yourself as it is possible you will not be able to fulfil those promises as your energy starts to calm down next year. It is a very exciting year and if you find that abundant opportunities and successes are coming your way, remain centred and focused until this pattern begins to slow down next year. It is very easy to trip up.

HEALTH RECOMMENDATIONS

Like the 3 House, this House is associated with the function of the liver and the gall-bladder. In addition to the health recommendations for the 3 House, remember to avoid burning out. If you recall from Chapter 2, the trigram for the 4 House is Sun where the lower line is broken (yin) leading into two yang upper lines. The weakness in this make-up is that you need fuelling and nourishment and support when you occupy this House as you lack any yang grounding.

Be particularly cautious of impetuous activities that could lead to accidents. These could either be self-inflicted or you could cause harm to others by 'skidding' out of control if you are not adequately centred while occupying this House.

Feng Shui Recommendations

✦

Your chi this year will be activated in the south-east sector of your property and since from an astrological perspective this House represents movement without stability, you do not need to over-emphasise the charge. A gentle, moving water feature could be used to activate this sector, or try an uplighter that is not too bright. Use any imagery that keeps you on track on your current journey. In this House you occupy a very favourable phase regarding movement and growth.

THE 5 SOIL HOUSE

INTERPRETATION

This is potentially the most powerful of all the 9 Houses as it represents the beginning and the end of a cycle. Remember that we are all born into this House and return here every nine years. Major turning points in our lives often occur in this House when we are 9, 18, 27, 36, 45, 54, 63, 72, 81, 90, 99 etc.

Whatever you initiate or create when you are in this House has the potential to have far reaching consequences —the effects could last up to nine years. Therefore, it is vitally important for you to use your best judgement in any new undertaking this year.

Old patterns, old relationships and even old health problems can be resolved. In fact, it is essential to deal with major issues. If you don't, the problems could linger another nine years!

LIFESTYLE RECOMMENDATIONS

Be very aware of the decomposing or destructive nature of being in the 5 House alongside the possibility for giving birth to a whole new future. Since your House occupies the centre this year, it would be wise to remain still – avoid making major moves or upheavals. In this House you receive the full force of your natal Star (your Principal Number) so focus on the things that will benefit your constitutional nature. By keeping still, you have more potential to do this.

HEALTH RECOMMENDATIONS

The centre in Chinese medicine is always associated with the Soil or Earth element which controls the function of the spleen, pancreas and stomach. In addition to the suggestions that I outline when occupying the 2 Soil House (also governing the function of the spleen, pancreas and stomach), there are other important steps to take.

It would be wise to initiate what I call a deep cleaning programme. In terms of Feng Shui this involves deep cleaning, spring cleaning or space clearing in your home environment.

In terms of your health pay more attention to your lymphatic system. A simple, easy and effective way to stimulate your lymphatic system, which is fundamentally sluggish by nature, is to rub your skin vigorously with a hot, damp towel every morning and evening. Always squeeze as much water out of the towel as possible and pay particular attention to the periphery of your body – feet and ankles, especially the toes, wrists, hands and fingers. Get right into the webbing between the fingers and toes.

Feng Shui Recommendations

✦

When you are occupying the centre of the system (every nine years), you need to bring elements of stability into your life. Since you are at the centre this year, you need to pay special attention to the centre of your home. Ideally, keep this area clutter free and if you find yourself travelling too much, being distracted by many different options, then bring an element of stability to the centre of your main space. For example, find some kind of statue or earthenware object that represents stability for you and place it either centrally in your main room or, if it is practical, at the centre of your home. Gold or yellow coloured table colourings in the middle of your room would also be auspicious.

THE 6 METAL HOUSE

INTERPRETATION

Here you will feel the full force of Heaven represented by the trigram Ch'ien which is made up of three yang unbroken lines. It is a very powerful House where much of what you have been working towards will start to bear fruit. This House represents harvest and a time for gathering. If what you have been working towards has been positive, you will reap its rewards; if you have been pursuing negative activities, then 'the chickens will come home to roost'.

The authority of 'Father' comes strongly into play when you occupy the 6 House. People around you will notice you, seek your advice, see you as an authority figure while at the same time, you will have a strong leaning toward feeling right most of the time. This clarity, coupled with a sense of justice, needs to be moderated a little otherwise people will find you overbearing or even dictatorial. Sometimes you will have little patience with those around you who seem to be struggling in the dark. Remember, they may be occupying a different House to you.

LIFESTYLE RECOMMENDATIONS

Stay on purpose with what you have been endeavouring to accomplish in the past few years. As you progress through the 6 Metal House, you will reap the benefits. This could be in terms of money, reputation or responsibility. Opportunities that come your way for raising your profile or taking on new positions of authority should be wisely accepted! Remember, those around you may not be having such a fulfilling year, so be careful not to cause jealousy or resentment among them by appearing too arrogant.

HEALTH RECOMMENDATIONS

The element Metal in Chinese medicine is associated with the functions of the lung and large intestine. Both are associated with gathering and absorbing and, at the same time, elimination. Keep active and be moderate in your eating and lifestyle. Excesses this year could cause you needless problems over the following two to three years.

Remember that this is a yang phase on the cycle which, on a health level, could mean that unresolved health issues are likely to solidify, calcify or stagnate. Typically, though, your health and chi will be positive and vibrant.

Feng Shui Recommendations

◆

Your chi has been charged from the north-west and the element is Metal. Since this House represents prosperity and the harvest, I would recommend placing three traditional Chinese coins tied together with red ribbon in the north-west sector of your home or the main room you occupy. Try not to over activate this area with Fire (Fire melts Metal); subtle, gentle lighting would be sufficient.

THE 7 METAL HOUSE

INTERPRETATION

This House represents the second phase of the harvest. Initially in the 6 House we gather in what we have sown and grown and now, in the 7 House, there are two more aspects of the harvest to see through. Firstly, once the harvest was stored, traditionally farmers would celebrate; hence this House is associated with joy. This is a chance to have fun, be irresponsible and let your hair down. The second and final phase in this process of harvesting is a quiet moment to reflect on what you may do in the future. Traditionally, all farmers did this by making a mental note of what they might do differently next year. You might like to plan for a quieter, more introspective, reflective phase in the second half of the year when you occupy the 7 Metal House.

LIFESTYLE RECOMMENDATIONS

For the initial part of this year, while your energy is in celebratory mode, remember that whatever you undertake in terms of work, new projects and even new relationships, they may all have a superficial quality. Ideas, plans, schemes and relationships initiated at this time may be short-lived and potentially trivial. Bear this in mind when considering any proposals that come your way.

Everyone can benefit from taking a break and letting their hair down. This would be an ideal time for that long-awaited and deserved holiday. At the same time, towards the end of this year, make time to prepare yourself for the next phase of the cycle, when you enter the 8 House next year.

HEALTH RECOMMENDATIONS

Like 6 Metal House, the organs to take particular care of are the lung and large intestine. Relaxing and being more self-indulgent than usual can cause more problems with the colon. Make a special effort to chew your food very, very well in this particular year. Avoid eating for an hour or two before you go to sleep. Any kind of exercise that stimulates both the gut and the lungs would be wise, such as rowing, cycling, push ups or an exercise class.

Feng Shui Recommendations

♦

Your chi is being charged from the west this year bringing with it a sense of relaxation, frivolity and celebration. Make the western sector of your main room or home as relaxing, comfortable and entertaining as possible. Lead quartz crystal in a west-facing window will help activate some of this charge.

THE 8 SOIL HOUSE

INTERPRETATION

The *I Ching* symbolism for this House is that of the Mountain. The image here is one of stillness, strength and durability. It is this stillness that can be unnerving while you occupy this House. You know that there is something in the air – it is the 9 Fire House, which is coming up next year. It is rather like that feeling of the calm before the storm in the tropics. It is an unsettling time.

In China, the image of the Mountain also has the added association that deep within the Mountain is a cave. When we occupy this House we tend to spend more time in our cave – being out of communication both in terms of hearing and being heard.

LIFESTYLE RECOMMENDATIONS

Make much more effort than usual to be extremely clear in all your communications while at the same time, pay far more attention to what is being said. Read the small print very carefully and make sure that your wishes and desires are communicated clearly. The reason for this is that you are in your 'cave' where normally you would expect to be heard easily. If you generally regard yourself as a good listener, be on your guard this year.

Despite the air of change and revolution that you notice, try not to initiate major upheavals during your occupancy of this House. Due to your reduced capacity to communicate, you could easily make a mistake that you might regret.

HEALTH RECOMMENDATIONS

Since you are occupying one of the more stagnant Houses and the element Soil governs the function of the spleen, pancreas and stomach, be extraordinarily careful not to over indulge. It is very easy this year to allow your health to go to seed. If you have a tendency to gain weight easily, make more effort than usual to exercise or cut down on foods that you know cause most problems.

The imagery of the Mountain is rather stoic and heavy. Try to avoid too many foods that have this kind of chi – heavy baked flour products, potatoes, pies, over-cooked foods and so on. Try to lighten your diet and incorporate plenty of freshness, variety and colour.

> # Feng Shui Recommendations
>
> ◆
>
> Since this year your chi is stronger in the north-east and you occupy the Mountain you need to bring in an element of stability and emptiness to allow deeper and fuller contemplation in your life. An empty vase, an empty trinket box or a cut lead quartz crystal bowl in this sector can strengthen your capacity to reflect and study.

THE 9 FIRE HOUSE

INTERPRETATION

When we occupy this House, our energy can be seen and noticed more than in any of the other eight. In Feng Shui, this southern sector is associated with our fame and recognition. In terms of astrology, it is about being recognised for whatever you have been doing. If you have been toiling hard at a new project, or you are looking to gain recognition at work, or you have some dark secret that you do not wish to have revealed, it all has the potential to come to the surface.

The Fire House is also associated with elimination, brightness and clarity. You may feel particularly inspired, active, outgoing, sociable and even independent. This is a very powerful year but do remember that it is swiftly followed by the quieter, cautious energy that will follow in the 1 Water House.

LIFESTYLE RECOMMENDATIONS

Use this year powerfully to publicise yourself. If you are looking to change your job, this is the year that you may get noticed. Your CV is likely to float to the top of the pile on a prospective employer's desk, or your tax return on the tax inspector's desk! Although you feel very energised, your chi has a diffusing, rather than consolidating, nature. The idea this year is to remain centred, focused and to avoid being too rash or impetuous. In short, be very careful not to burn out.

HEALTH RECOMMENDATIONS

Fire is the element in Chinese medicine associated with the function of the heart and small intestine. Very good support for the heart at this time is to bring a sense of 'rhythm' into your life. Dashing about from one appointment to another, taking on dozens of new projects simultaneously may seem appropriate while you occupy the Fire House but this erratic use of your time and energy is potentially damaging to the heart. Therefore, bring a sense of discipline and rhythm into your daily life.

The element Fire can bring with it surprises. Be particularly careful to avoid burns, scalds or electrical shocks. Remember that fire needs fuel and for all of us, this means taking care of our diet and adding discipline and rhythm to meal times. Try to avoid snacking on the run and make time to be centred and focus on regular, wholesome meals.

Feng Shui Recommendations

✦

Your chi is being charged actively by the south and with the Fire that the sun brings. Activate this southern sector this year with candles, uplighters or colours that reflect any hue of Fire – purples, burgundies, reds, pinks and even orange. In terms of career, place any certificates or awards in this sector of your office to remind you of your continued success.

Chapter Six

Directionology

WE HAVE ALL INTUITIVELY made successful journeys in our lives, whether short or long, that in hindsight seemed effortless, whether this was a short weekend visit to an old friend, a holiday abroad or a major move such as a change of job, home or country. Without any real effort on our part, the journey benefited us immensely. On the other hand, we can all recall journeys that were incredibly fraught and which we later regretted. It was as if we were swimming against the tide, encountering lots of small irritating problems, big obstacles, accidents, illnesses and maybe even losing a job. If you practise the system that I outline in this chapter, it will help you to time the major moves in your life – such as emigrating or moving house – so that you go with the Tao rather than against it. When you have mastered the system, look back at major life moves and see if it ties up. Having the winds, tides and currents in your favour makes any journey more effortless and enjoyable.

In China, where 9-House Astrology is still practised, it is used primarily in connection with spatial Feng Shui. The main emphasis is on determining which House you will occupy in any given month, day or year, and applying Feng Shui remedies to achieve the best result. In Japan, where 9-Star Ki Astrology is currently very popular, Directionology plays a far bigger role. Not only do they attach importance to your horoscope and the House you occupy in any given month, day or

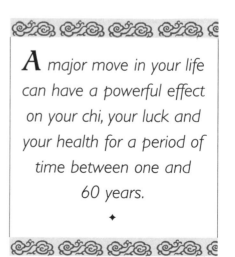

A major move in your life can have a powerful effect on your chi, your luck and your health for a period of time between one and 60 years.

✦

year, much importance is also given to the direction that you take towards, for example, a new job, interview, holiday or house move.

In this chapter, I will show you how to avoid certain directions based on the year in question. A major move in your life can have a powerful effect on your chi, your luck and your health for a period of time between one and 60 years. Whether the move is 100 metres, 100 miles or 1000 miles it makes no difference – you have still moved yourself and your chi in a particular direction. Moves that you make within a particular month have a less enduring effect but can still cause disruption for a period of between one month and 60 months. This calculation is explained in my earlier book, *Feng Shui Astrology*. It is also possible to use 9-Star Ki Astrology to determine the most auspicious time for short trips, holidays and business appointments where the length of time is less than two months. In this case the calculation must be made based around the day in question. The same principles apply but the after effects of an inauspicious move are only felt for up to 60 days. This could mean being left disorientated, isolated, low in stamina or simply run down. For details of this more complex calculation, I refer you to the *Yearly Almanac* produced by J. Higa listed in the resource section at the back of the book.

HOW TO USE THIS SYSTEM

STEP 1
You must first establish which star is at the centre of the Lo Shu Magic Square for the year in question. For a quick reference guide, check the chart on page 72. Remember, that the year in question always begins on 4th February and ends on 3rd February the following year. In this example I have chosen the 9 square which also represents the year 2000.

STEP 2
Now establish where your Principal Star sits within the year in question. Using the example of a 9 Fire year, check the diagram on page 87 to find your Star.

STEP 3
When you look more closely at the diagrams on page 87, be clear about the directions involved. These are the cardinal points of north, south, east and west together with the intercardinal points of north-east, north-west, south-east and south-west. The Chinese tend to divide these points equally by 45 degrees, as I have illustrated, whereas the Japanese prefer to narrow down the field for the cardinal directions to

30 degrees and broaden out the intercardinal directions to 60 degrees. The thinking behind this difference is that there is a more powerful, concentrated (yang) charge along the cardinal directions.

STEP 4

When I refer to directions using this system, it is important to bear in mind that they all pass through the centre. For example, if you were a Number 4 Star, and I explained that it would be wise to avoid moving west that particular year, you would be drawing a line through the Magic Square from east to west passing through the centre.

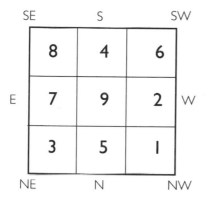

Magic square for '9' year
4 February 2000 - 3 February 2001

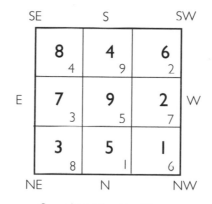

Superimposing the '9' year
onto the Lo Shu magic square

DIRECTIONS TO AVOID

TO GIVE YOU AN opportunity to practise this system as I explain it, we will assume the year being a 9 Fire year and that the star in question is a 3 Tree.

TOWARDS YOUR STAR

If you refer back to the diagram above, you will notice that the 3 Tree Star is occupying the north-east in a 9 year. This means that, in this particular example, a move towards the north-east is a move towards your own Star.

The reason for avoiding this direction is that you are likely to move into yourself. This could make you more isolated, with the consequence that you will be out of communication with those around you. If either logically or intuitively you planned to move in this direction, perhaps because you felt it could increase your chances of recognition, heighten your profile in your career, or to help you move out of isolation, it would be a major mistake. A move towards yourself is best avoided if you wish to remain active, outgoing and sociable.

AWAY FROM YOUR STAR

Taking the example of a 3 Tree Star in a 9 Fire year, then this is a move towards the south-west.

The symbolism here is that you are moving away from yourself, your intuition and your own natal Star. The likely outcome is that you will lose track, focus and direction in your life. You are likely to procrastinate and miss opportunities. This is not a wise direction if you wish to remain on purpose and clear in your direction.

TOWARDS THE 5 YELLOW STAR

All stars need to be careful of a move towards the 5 Yellow Star. In a 9 Fire year, it is occupying the 1 House which is in the north.

The 5 Yellow Star is associated with danger. A move towards the 5 Yellow Star is a direct move towards what I call 'obvious danger'. This could be a move or a situation where you already knew the pitfalls and dangers in advance. For example, you were warned by a surveyor that there was rot in the roof timbers, but you still went ahead without heeding the advice. Another example could be a move to a new home which also involves a change of job when you knew ahead of time that you might miss out on enhancing your career, or that you may lose some existing clients. When you move towards the 5 Yellow Star it symbolises the obvious, and not the hidden, dangers that may lie ahead.

AWAY FROM THE 5 YELLOW STAR

In the case of a 9 Fire Year, when the 5 Yellow Star is occupying the north, it indicates a move for all of us towards the south. Here, the danger that the 5 Yellow Star symbolises is no longer ahead of you but behind you, at your back. Of all the moves, this is potentially the most dangerous. For the other directions that I have outlined, you could be forewarned and potentially forearmed to deal with them. With this one, you would have to be a Samurai with eyes in the back of your head to cope! Danger from the unexpected could involve an accident, loss of business, degeneration of your health, breakdown of a relationship or being robbed or attacked.

5 YELLOW STAR IN THE CENTRE

Years when the 5 Yellow Star is occupying the centre are, for all of us, times of major change, re-invention, new beginnings and ending past patterns. When the 5 Yellow Star is in the centre, we are all in our own unique House. At that time, it is wise to remain still and benefit from the charge that we each uniquely receive by being in our own House.

It is worth noting that humanity has gone through major global changes at the following times, which were all 5 Yellow Soil years. These were 1914 – the outbreak of World War I, 1941 – the Japanese bombing of Pearl Harbour and the USA's entry into World War II, 1950 – the Chinese invasion of Tibet and the Korean War, 1968 – student riots in Europe and the USA. More recently, in 1995 the resolution of the Yugoslav conflict with the signing of the Dayton Agreement. The year 2004 is the next 5 Yellow Soil year on the horizon.

YOUR STAR IN THE CENTRE

When your Star occupies the centre of the Magic Square, it is a time of rebirth and of breaking away from patterns of the past. We are all born into this year and pass through it when we are aged 9, 18, 27, 36, 45, 54, 63, and so on. The wisdom of 9-Star Ki Astrology suggests that you should remain centred and still at this time even though you may feel distracted by all the opportunities for change that may come your way. Being at the centre in this particular year does allow opportunities for change to gravitate towards you more powerfully than in any other year. It is wise, however, to stay still and benefit from the charge that you receive by being at the centre.

CONCLUSION

I believe that Directionology plays a vital part in your journey using Feng Shui. Before you get overly concerned or neurotic about the possible dangers of a wrong move, do check back into your own life to see if a pattern emerges. I have spent many years reading and researching into the lives of historical and contemporary people and can validate what I have just shown you. Once you have a sense of 'who the person is' (their Principal Star) and 'where they are' (which House they occupy in any given year), it is fairly easy to show the effect of Directionology by any moves the individual might have made, such as emigrating, or making a career change. My conclusion is that many famous and successful individuals in our time, who are completely unaware of this system, have simply made the right move in the right direction at the right time! You now have the upper hand to benefit from this timeless yet elegant system.

FENG SHUI AND YOUR HEALTH

Inner Feng Shui

Chapter Seven

The Five Elements and Self Assessment

SANDWICHED BETWEEN Heaven and Earth, it is you who is the vital factor as far as successful Feng Shui is concerned. Given that you now know who you are, where you are and which directions to plan regarding any move on your journey, it is vital to your progress with Feng Shui that you understand your own inner Feng Shui. Our inner world reveals our current health and which of the Five Elements may need support through, for example, lifestyle, activity and diet.

In Part 2, I took you through the first step on your Feng Shui journey which was to assess who and where you are using astrology. That information is vital for your successful navigation on this journey. In Part 4 we will take a closer look at your immediate environment – your home – and see what support you can bring in to strengthen your health, vision and success in life. Here, I will concentrate on the most important aspect of your journey, you, and in particular your relationship with your immediate environment, your health and your relationships with others.

As with the sections on astrology and Feng Shui, this part of the book will also be based around the central theme of Chinese thought, which is the dynamics and interactions of yin and yang and the Five Elements. The holistic perspective that we find in Chinese medicine is mirrored in astrology and in our practise of spatial Feng Shui. Everything is interconnected. The mind, body and spirit do not operate as separate entities. Every aspect of our lives is mirrored in some other shape or form, whether this is in terms of our health, relationships or the home, they are all deeply intertwined.

Western medicine, which is primarily driven by Carthesian and Newtonian science, is designed to work directly on the symptoms. Chinese medicine on the other hand, has, for thousands of years, been engaged in the deeper enquiry into the cause of the symptoms. For decades, the West has been largely seduced, enthralled and won over by the symptoms-based approach. It is also obvious that much contemporary interest in Feng Shui is driven by the desire to achieve results instantly, also using a more symptomatic approach. Working with the cause of the imbalance in our life makes more demands on our time and effort. It can reveal to us that the cause is mirrored in many other facets of our life. As a Feng Shui practitioner, with a background in Oriental medicine, it has been my experience that what most clients see as a 'problem' is also represented in many other facets of their life. Feng Shui, for them, is often simply a new tool to try to fix an old problem. Suddenly, their home is to blame for all of their problems! Closer enquiries can often reveal previous problems with their job, health, diet, relationship with parents or children, or an inability to handle pressure. In all these situations, outside factors are frequently blamed.

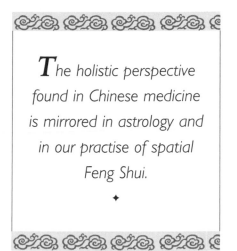

The holistic perspective found in Chinese medicine is mirrored in astrology and in our practise of spatial Feng Shui.

♦

I will use the model of the Five Elements as the background for assessing your current health and showing how you can strengthen this through changes in diet, lifestyle and exercise. By recognising what we need to work on within ourselves, we have greater potential to harness our intuition and far greater possibilities to achieve our dreams with the use of spatial Feng Shui. Identifying areas of weakness using Oriental Diagnosis can then lead us to 'support' this element, not only through the use of this inner Feng Shui but also with the additional support of spatial Feng Shui.

WHAT IS HEALTH?

I BELIEVE THAT THE QUALITY of our health provides the foundation for understanding Feng Shui and putting it into practice in an effective way. We primarily draw on our vitality and indeed our 'inspiration' when we decide to bring about changes in ourselves, our lives and our environment. Our judgement and our perception of what we believe to be best for us is coloured by our current state of health. Any imbalances within us will naturally reflect how we see the world around us and how we choose to react. On all levels, the quality of our health will colour our outlook, intuition, dream, practice of Feng Shui, relationships and our journey.

We all know that our health is in a constant state of change. Some days we are lively and enthusiastic, whereas at other times we can feel despondent and have difficulty in seeing fresh possibilities in our lives. What we can relate to is that health is dynamic and, rather like our environment, is constantly changing. Using the principles of Chinese medicine, it is possible to realise that our body and our health simply mirror the environment that we live in. When we line up our dream and our internal condition with the external expression of Feng Shui, we have the powerful possibility to bring about long term and potent success in the use of spatial Feng Shui.

ENVIRONMENT

THE BASIS OF OUR HEALTH essentially begins here. The environment in this context covers all the aspects that surround us that provide us with immediate sustenance. There are yin/yang varieties of these different so-called 'foods' that supply us. To begin with, on a yin vibrational level, the factors that can support us or hinder us on our journey include Feng Shui, Geopathic Stress, Electro Magnetic Stress, chi and our climate.

Supporting yourself with powerful Feng Shui, while at the same time neutralising the harmful effects of any Geopathic Stress or Electro Magnetic Stress in your environment, are the first steps to undertake. Working with the existing quality of chi in your environment or changing it or moving to a more suitable location that has the kind of chi that you need, all need to be considered. You cannot change the climate, but without a doubt it has an enormous bearing on how you feel. You can, however, begin to change your internal climate, which can make you more comfortable wherever you choose to live. For example, to offset a predominantly cold or damp climate, you could incorporate more of the element Fire into your cooking, by using a high flame, and short, sharp cooking styles like stir-fry. You will then feel far more comfortable than living on raw foods, raw fruits and cold liquids. Similarly, you could bring Fire into your home environment, by using bright lighting or candles, or bright colours such as red, purple, pink or orange.

The quality of the air that you breathe is drawn immediately from your environment. Obviously, the fresher and cleaner the air, the better you feel. Without moving to the Swiss mountains, what can you do to enhance the quality of the air that you breathe? You could take more exercise, allowing more oxygenation to occur within the body, you could sleep with the window slightly open and encourage your colleagues at work to improve the ventilation and so bring fresh air into the work place.

While the vibrational qualities of Feng Shui, chi, the climate and air are intangible and express the yin qualities that we absorb on a daily basis, our intake of water and food represent the more tangible yang qualities. We have far more control over these two factors. Given that our body is made up of some 60 per cent fluid, it is important to replenish it with the best quality water that nature can provide. I personally favour using the best water that I can find for cooking, preparing beverages and simply to drink. Practically speaking, this is freshly bottled spring water. It is not just the chemistry of the water that I am concerned with but the chi it provides. There is no comparison between metropolitan treated water and the water that is available direct from a source.

The other main component that we take on board on a daily basis is food. Again, it not just the chemical composition of the foods that is so important but the chi that it provides. Is the food fresh? Does it have chi? Does it provide us with chi? What is cooked with chi? The most important factor to remember when you look at your daily food is that you have complete control over what you eat and how it is prepared. In many ways this is not true for the other three components that we draw from our environment – environmental chi, air and water.

BLOOD

The quality of our blood, both on a biochemical and chi level, is drawn principally from the factors that I have just outlined. In Chinese medicine, blood is viewed as the synthesis of the immediate environment. Naturally, the quality of what we have absorbed in terms of chi, air, liquid and food has a direct effect on the blood. For centuries poets and writers have acknowledged the external expression of their characters by linking them with metaphorical descriptions of their blood, such as being cold-blooded, hot-blooded, bloody-minded, bloodthirsty, young blood and having aristocratic blood.

ORGANS

For centuries, Chinese medicine has taken the view that our health is due primarily to the harmony and function of our internal organs. Again, there is this acknowledgement that the environment creates our blood, and that our blood creates and nourishes our internal organs. Although these various organs play different roles in the body, they are rather like individual musicians within an orchestra. The overall expression of the orchestra (our body and our health) is at its most powerful when everyone knows what they are doing and each musician is performing well.

However, it only takes one instrument within an orchestra to be flat or out of harmony and the whole orchestra will be affected. In Chinese medicine, the five main players are the heart, the spleen/pancreas, the lungs, the kidneys and the liver. These five are all linked with the Five Elements and also have smaller 'instruments' that support them, including the small intestine, stomach, colon, bladder, reproductive system and gall-bladder.

HEALTH

Our health is ultimately the product of our environment. It is born out of the quality and function of our internal organs and the quality of blood that we have created. Health, in this context, begins to take on a much broader meaning as our environment includes the emotions we experience, the stresses we endure and the relationships we are involved in. Good health, therefore, must encompass our consciousness, our awareness and most importantly, our ability to respond to challenges. Obviously, there are no quick-fix solutions.

THE DISCHARGE AND ELIMINATION PROCESS

Chinese medicine is always looking to bring about change on a deep level and this naturally differs with the more symptomatic or superficial approach that some forms of healing may take. Any big change in our lifestyle, Feng Shui, diet and routine are naturally going to cause different levels of discomfort. The more violent and radical the changes are, the more likely they are to cause some kind of reaction. Provided you stay focused on your journey, you can ride out the discomforts when they occur. It is very common for some people to be perturbed by the level of reaction to change that they feel, both physically and mentally, and to simply return to their old route or previous patterns. By seeing these violent reactions as part of the process of change, we can better tolerate and understand them and see them as short-term reactions.

The kinds of symptoms that can occur when you bring about change to your inner Feng Shui include aches and pains, tiredness, chills and fevers. Your energy levels can appear to be erratic – at times you may crave more sleep than usual and you may show less of an inclination to socialise. Basically, your body is internalising its focus to bring about deep and profound changes. Old, unwanted excess baggage can surface and this can present itself as minor aches and pains, chills and fevers, coughs and some irregularity with the bowels. As if this is not enough to contend with, deep-seated emotions can start to appear and colour your immediate outlook.

These can include feeling fearful, cautious, irritable, impatient, hysterical, despondent, depressed, mistrusting and cynical.

I always view the discharge and elimination process as profoundly helpful on our journey, provided we do not get attached to what we are eliminating! At the end of the day, it is the past and unwanted baggage. While we are involved in this elimination process, our whole vision and world narrows down, in a process I call 'the duvet syndrome'. When you feel unwell, perhaps suffering from a fever and a cough, and you take yourself to bed for a day or two, you may notice that your universe ends at the foot of the bed. You are completely caught up in your own personal suffering and you have no interest in what is going on in the world beyond your bedroom. Our behaviour in the world at large when we are going through a big change is equally self-indulgent. It is important, however, that it is self-indulgent. There are two things to bear in mind:

1. Remember to avoid all the factors that have built up to lead to this discharge in the first place

2. Realise that this is the first stage in developing a new future for yourself.

Undoubtedly there are 'quick-fix' symptom-based approaches to all areas of life including Feng Shui and health. Such rapid remedies provide almost instant results. Deeper changes will always bring to the surface all the underlying chaos but, in the long term, these changes will be profound and have a longer-lasting effect. Provided the changes are well thought out, well administered and reviewed from time to time, your journey is likely to be far more stable and rewarding.

GUIDELINES FOR YOUR WELL-BEING

1. TAKE THE BIG VIEW

The fascination I have with Feng Shui, Chinese medicine and associated healing arts is how they are all intertwined philosophically. The easiest way to appreciate all these systems is to start with the broadest possible perspective. Having a 'macroscopic view' when dealing with any of the related issues gives you greater insight when you begin to work with the 'microscopic' remedies. Rather than getting caught up in detail, try to see these aspects within the context of the whole picture. For example, in astrology it is easier to see 'where you are' within a bigger cycle of change. As far as your health is concerned, begin to see how minor imbalances with your inner Feng Shui can relate to your physical well-being. As far as spatial Feng Shui is concerned, remember that every sector of your home, the layout of the desk, the clutter in the car and the Feng Shui of the working environment, all need to be considered as part of making changes in your life overall. I often meet individuals who have put into effect brilliant Feng Shui remedies in their home but failed to mirror these in other areas of their lives.

2. BE FLEXIBLE/ADAPTABLE

Living as we do, in a changing world, it is important that we learn how to be sufficiently physically and emotionally flexible to cope. As human beings, we have survived thousands of years of evolution while other species have become extinct. The main reason for this is the special strength that we all inherently have which allows us to adapt to change. We are not, nor do we wish to be, dinosaurs! The primary reason for their extinction was their inability to adapt to the violent changes in their environment.

The pessimistic view is that the world we live in will become much more challenging in the future. We are all sitting on a potential time bomb in terms of environmental disasters, economic decline, social and spiritual chaos, diseases, droughts and starvation. We all know that prevention is the key to resolving these issues. Deep down, however, we know that even if positive changes were made today, it would take decades before some sense of balance returned. The unpleasant truth is that the global situation at present is far more likely to get worse before it gets any better. To survive this era in humanity's progress, we will need to become flexible and adaptable.

For the body, this means exercises that keep us not only in shape but loose and supple. As far as the mind and spirit is concerned, it is important to develop a spirit of openness and an appetite to find out more – especially other peoples' ideas and perspectives. The worst thing any of us could do to this timeless body of knowledge that we call Feng Shui would be to turn it into dogma!

3. SHOW INTEGRITY

This is basically a yin/yang approach to both seeing and appreciating life within and around us. When we appreciate that all phenomena are interconnected, then it is far easier to realise the importance of sorting out issues in our lives that may well be reflected on many different levels including emerging as health problems. For example, if we are looking for wealth, it is simply not enough to place 'quick fix' remedies in the wealth sector of the home, office or garden. We need to be looking at the whole issue of wealth in our lives and begin to notice where there may be a blockage or some incompletion that is hindering us. Do we owe somebody some money, either currently or from the past? Until some attempt is made to sort this out it will hold us back. Look at any health problems in the same way. Is a problem at work literally giving you a pain in the neck for example?

4. AVOID COMPLAINING

Sharp outbursts of complaining are pretty good for the system! There is nothing wrong with 'venting your spleen'! However, chronic complaining is a different story altogether. I know many individuals who are never fully self-expressed until they are complaining on all four cylinders. It seems to lighten them up and inspire them somehow.

The problem with chronic complaining is that we are cleverly avoiding responsibility for many areas of our lives. We can become very good at reasoning why it is not our problem and, while doing so, we are cleverly avoiding admitting any responsibility. Unless we accept changes in our lives and bear the responsibility for their success or failure, our progress on this journey is limited. I have had countless telephone enquiries from potential clients wanting their homes 'Feng Shuid' while at the same time complaining about two or three other consultants who had done the job before and it had not worked! These are the jobs that I skilfully avoid as I have no desire to be complaint number three or four on their list while at the same time, I realise that there is a high expectation on their part to 'fix' their life.

5. GIVE MORE THAN YOU RECEIVE

Our natural environment is extraordinarily generous. In the rare moments when we are still and at peace, we can truly sense the timeless gift of nature that surrounds us all. A wise, traditional farmer anywhere in the world would plant excess seed to allow for insects and birds to take their share. A wise farmer would also take what was needed from the plants and make every effort to support and replenish them.

Giving and receiving are yin/yang related activities. The act of giving to others – whether in terms of time, space, ideas, love or material possessions – creates the space for you to receive something in return. When we are completely focused on ourselves and forget to 'discharge' some of our energy into the world, we just get stuck. There is no room for inspiration or creativity and stubborn illnesses or debilitating fatigue can often result. The act of giving simply creates the space for new opportunities and new possibilities to enter your life.

THE FIVE ELEMENTS

AS I HAVE EXPLAINED earlier the Five Element System is central to all aspects of Oriental philosophy including Feng Shui and 9-Star Astrology and it is just as important in Chinese medicine. The same interactions and interplay are involved and in this section I will concentrate on their relevance to your health and any changes you need to take on board. Later on in this chapter, and in the following chapter, when I outline the recommendations I will be encouraging you to:

1. Identify which of the elements is currently weak

and

2. Show you how to strengthen that element by giving the previous one support.

This is only one angle that you could take using this dynamic but it is the simplest and easiest to start with. If, for example, you identify in the self-assessment section at the end of this chapter, that the Fire element (heart/small intestine) is your weak element then I will be encouraging you to strengthen and motivate the previous one, the Tree/Wood element in Chapter 7.

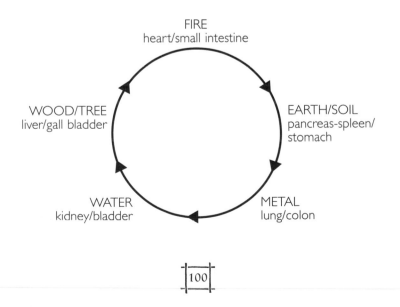

As with spatial Feng Shui, it is important to remember to work with all the sectors to some degree and simply emphasise the area that you wish to bring more focus to. The same principle applies here. There will be ideas in Chapter 7 which relate to all the elements and they will all provide you with valuable hints and tips. However, pay special attention to giving support to the element that shows up as being the weakest.

THE FIVE MAJOR PLAYERS

WE ARE NOW AT A stage where it is possible to look at the function and nature of each of the Five Elements in relation to the major internal organs. From the perspective that our environment creates our blood, which nourishes the internal organs, which in turn filter and recreate the blood, it is these vital organs that provide the final link to our health and consciousness. With a little bit of background knowledge from the Western and Oriental point of view, you will begin to grasp the essence of 'inner Feng Shui'. Once you have assessed yourself at the end of this Chapter, you will have the opportunity in Chapter 7 to strengthen any weak element or elements using a variety of approaches including Feng Shui, exercises and meditation.

To help you get the most from the next section, on Oriental Diagnosis, it would be useful to look at the organs involved in the Five Elements from an Oriental perspective, both in terms of structure and function as well as their energetic nature. Naturally, each of these major organs plays a vital energetic role in terms of your inner Feng Shui and working with them effectively helps to balance your inner and outer worlds. An overview of these players will help you decide in Part 5 what support you can build in on your journey.

WATER ELEMENT: KIDNEYS (BLADDER AND REPRODUCTIVE SYSTEM)

PHYSIOLOGY AND FUNCTION

These remarkable organs, each weighing only 5 ounces, play a magnificent role in balancing the body's complex chemicals, continuously cleaning and filtering the blood and removing potentially life-threatening waste products. Within the kidneys there are a million filtering devices known as nephrons. These tiny tubules interface with the blood as it passes through the kidneys and filter out waste products, re-absorbing some 99 per cent of the fluid and returning vitamins, hormones, glucose and amino acids to the bloodstream. The kidneys work remarkably hard. They manage to filter twice the volume of your blood in just one hour. It is easy to think that the digestive system is our main route for disposing of waste within the body. In fact, the kidneys do far more of this process. The kidneys also control the volume of water within the blood and make sure that the blood does not become too alkaline or acidic. In the process of breaking down amino acids, the waste substance urea is produced and must be dealt with by the kidneys. Too much urea in the blood is extremely harmful. The function of the kidneys is closely linked to the liver – which, coincidentally is supported by Wood, the next element on the Five Element cycle.

INNER FENG SHUI

The kidneys are the source of our will – providing us with endurance, stamina and courage. From an Oriental perspective, the kidneys are seen as the channel through which our constitution is formed, creating a direct link between us, our parents and our ancestors. Within the cycle of human development, they are related to our birth, childhood and maturation. Part of this development is the creation of our bones, energetically controlled by the function of the kidneys. Strong teeth and bones are both symptomatic of constitutionally strong kidneys.

SUPPORT

Warm or hot foods are preferable to cold or frozen food products. Hot drinks are better than highly chilled ones. Moderately salty or savoury foods are also beneficial. The kidneys, being governed by the element Water, which can be synonymous with the night and the winter, benefit from plenty of sleep and periods of dormancy to recharge. Being in 'hyper' mode for days and nights on end can temporarily exhaust the kidneys. Drawing on high levels of adrenaline also drains and damages kidney essence.

Physical activity that induces sweating is beneficial because this form of elimination can relieve some of the load on the kidneys. Excessive sexual energy and a high dependency on adrenaline exhausts the kidneys. Environments that are very wet or cold or damp do not benefit the kidneys. These organs prefer stability in our lives and it is important for their energetic well-being that you maintain stability in your home, work and relationships. Changing your home, job or relationships is often 'unsettling' for the kidneys.

FIRE ELEMENT: HEART (SMALL INTESTINE)

PHYSIOLOGY AND FUNCTION

Roughly the size of a clenched fist, the heart is a dynamic pump that moves the blood around the body and to the lungs. The sheer volume of blood that is pumped is amazing – 4000 gallons over a 24 hour period. This is equivalent to moving blood some 60,000 miles through the veins, arteries and capillaries. The muscles of the heart are Herculean in their strength, pumping with tremendous force at an average of 70 times per minute, which can increase to 160 times per minute or more and slow down as low as 50 times per minute when resting. Being so active, the heart requires more than 10 times as much nourishment from the blood as the other organs and tissues in the body. The heart draws this nourishment from the blood via the coronary arteries. The build-up of fatty deposits in the coronary arteries can cause them to become blocked, which in turn kills off a portion of the muscle required for the heart to pump efficiently. Minimising the risk of this occurring is a major problem in the West, where one in four individuals suffers from some form of heart disease.

INNER FENG SHUI

From an Oriental perspective, the heart not only governs the blood and the vessels for transporting the blood, but also the mind, or what the Chinese call 'Shen'. The mind, in this context, is connected with our sensitivity on a vibrational level with our outside world, our memory, our thinking and our self-awareness. Powerful Shen helps to keep us calm, feel tuned in to our environment and intuitive. When the Shen is well regulated, our response to the outside world is calm, relaxed and reasonable. However, when out of balance, it can create behaviour that is irrational and hysterical and we can become forgetful and hypersensitive.

SUPPORT

Fire, left to its own devices, can be very undisciplined. It needs a hearth, regulation of oxygen, some kind of stability in order not to burn out of control. Therefore, a lifestyle that has a reasonable amount of order, pace and structure is beneficial. Erratic and inconsistent use of your energy weakens the Fire. Since this is a naturally warm element, it is best to support it and activities such as socialising, dancing, singing, laughter and humour are all beneficial. Physical activity that involves the upper part of the body – the lungs and the arms are important to strengthen this region. In terms of Feng Shui, living in a home that has stability, that is warm and welcoming does much to support Fire. Living alone, or without sufficient interaction with others does not feed the Fire nature. Having an undisciplined and chaotic working or social life does not help either.

METAL ELEMENT: LUNGS (COLON)

PHYSIOLOGY AND FUNCTION

Unlike the heart, the lungs do not have muscles of their own to control breathing. There is a small vacuum in the chest allowing contraction and expansion to occur as the diaphragm and chest muscles create the dynamic force needed for breathing. The most important work of the lungs is done by the alveoli which are small, cherry shaped sacs at the very end of the air passages. The total surface area of these alveoli in both lungs would be equivalent to a tennis ball. Each alveolus connects with minute capillaries carrying blood pumped from the heart. Through its tiny membrane, the capillary can discharge carbon dioxide from the blood to the lungs. Cells within the blood then return oxygen, re-charging it before returning it to the heart.

Each gentle intake of breath has a volume of about 1 litre. The total capacity of the lungs is more like eight times this amount, however. Lying still requires the use of some 18 litres of air per minute, sitting requires 32 litres, walking would need 56 litres, whereas running would need between 100 and 112 litres of air per minute. Although the lungs are 'internal organs' – they are housed within the body – they are effectively on the surface. Like their partner, the colon, they interface directly with the external environment. This means the lungs are especially vulnerable to environmental hazards. Nicotine, carbon dioxide, lead, nitrogen dioxide and benzopyrene are extremely dangerous in excess for the health of the lungs.

INNER FENG SHUI

In Oriental medicine, the lungs are regarded both as an absorbing and eliminating organ. The lungs are understood to govern the outside of the body – the skin. In fact, skin is often referred to as the third lung. Where the heart controls our mental and emotional awareness of the outside world, the lungs control our physical awareness. This is primarily through the senses of touch, taste, smell, and hearing.

SUPPORT

Since the element Metal is concerned with contraction, focus and intensity, it would be wise not to over emphasise these qualities in your life. Being under intense pressure, both physically and emotionally, or feeling trapped in a situation, damages the lung energetically. Being able to communicate freely and to get things 'off your chest' are valuable releases for lung energy. Physical activity that makes you breathless and induces sweating is also important. Plenty of fresh air, both at home and at work is essential. A badly oxygenated living, working or sleeping environment can easily bring about feelings of depression and despair. Surrounding yourself with plenty of healthy green plants at home is also beneficial.

SOIL/EARTH ELEMENT: SPLEEN/PANCREAS (STOMACH)

PHYSIOLOGY AND FUNCTION

The pancreas is like a factory that provides energy for almost every cell or organ in the body. Although only 6 ins (15 cms) long and weighing about 3 ounces, the pancreas is probably the most active organ in the body. It has two major tasks, the first is to create the hormone insulin, a chemical that is essential to our survival. Insulin regulates blood levels of glucose, which provides the body with energy and is the basic nutrient of the cells. Secondly, the pancreas produces approximately 1 litre a day of digestive enzymes, which alkalise the semi-digested acidic food as it passes from the stomach into the digestive tract. The most critical role that the pancreas plays is in the production of insulin. Without this hormone, glucose levels in the blood would go out of control leading to diabetes, which if unchecked can lead to serious illness. Excess glucose in the blood (in a healthy person) is passed on to the liver and muscles where it is stored as glycogen and can be called upon when needed.

The spleen has two major functions. Firstly, it acts as a filter to remove worn-out, defective or misshapen red blood cells from the bloodstream. Its second function is connected with the immune system. One of the main defences against infection within the body is provided by what is called lymphoid tissue. The adenoids and tonsils are also lymphoid tissues. The spleen is by far the largest lymphoid organ and produces some of the antibodies, lymphocytes and phagocytes that destroy infectious micro-organisms such as bacteria and viruses.

INNER FENG SHUI

Although these are two distinctly separate organs from a Western perspective, they are regarded as one in traditional Chinese Medicine. The spleen in particular is seen as the central and commanding organ regarding digestion and the creation of blood. In the rural, agricultural setting of traditional China, the imagery given to the spleen was that of a storehouse for grain within the community. Grain would be harvested on outlying farms and brought to the storehouse where it was cleaned, stored and distributed as and when it was needed. The element Soil which governs these organs is also 'central' to the body and the way it controls stability and distribution. Apart from the imagery of storage, Chinese medical texts also emphasise the function of transportation and transformation. Energetically, the spleen/pancreas governs the function of our intellect – our powers of concentration, analysis and study.

SUPPORT

If you were to make a comparison between the Soil element and an attribute of our behaviour, then the phrase 'completion' would summarise it well. Making the effort to complete tasks in your life benefits the spleen and pancreas. Taking care of all outstanding issues could involve finishing projects, paying bills, fulfilling promises, dealing with unfinished conversations or unresolved conflicts. On a physical level, activities that bring you near to the earth such as gardening, digging, walking all help to nurture this Soil element. The most nurturing activity of all would be to spend 10 – 15 minutes per day barefoot on the earth allowing this natural charge to support you. The meridians (or channels) of chi energy connected with the spleen and pancreas are found in both big toes and run along the edge of the feet towards the ankle.

WOOD/TREE ELEMENT: LIVER (GALL-BLADDER)

PHYSIOLOGY AND FUNCTION

Weighing about 3 pounds (1.4 kilograms) and tucked up beneath the diaphragm on the right hand side of the body is the liver – the biggest organ of the body. The liver has over 500 functions and a failure of any of these would spell disaster for us. Over 1000 enzymes are produced by the liver to cope with all the chemical conversions that the body needs. Of all the major organs of the body, the liver is the only one that can regenerate itself in just a few months. The liver can still function with 85 per cent of its active cells destroyed or with up to 80 per cent having been surgically removed. One of its main functions is to provide the constituents for the building of red blood cells. Even the waste from this process is recycled to make bile – the digestive enzyme that is passed to the gall-bladder – which in turn helps to break down fat in the digestive process based in the duodenum.

If there is too much glucose in the blood, the liver can convert this to glycogen, storing it and releasing it as a fuel for the muscles of the body. When we exercise vigorously, we produce the waste product lactic acid, which can be harmful to the body. The liver recycles this chemical as glycogen for storage and release on future occasions. The liver also converts toxins in the blood into harmless chemicals that can be removed from the body, and controls blood levels of amino acids, converting some into proteins, some into glucose, and the rest into urea to be passed to the kidneys for excretion from the body.

INNER FENG SHUI

In Oriental healing, the liver is seen as the home of our spirit or chi. It is responsible for our motivation, flexibility and growth. There is an interesting parallel between Oriental healing and Western medicine regarding the supportive nature of the liver towards the heart. The liver can act as a safety and release valve for blood passing towards the heart. A massive vein on the top portion of the liver (hepatic vein) passes directly to the heart and if there was a sudden release of blood in the circulatory system that could well swamp the heart, then the liver steps in by holding on to the extra blood like the sluice gates on a reservoir. The liver can then release this blood slowly when the heart is ready to take the additional flow.

In some traditional texts, the liver is regarded as the General of the body – creating order and harmony throughout the system. Flexible and light-spirited describes the healthy condition of the liver. The liver also rules the muscles and tendons of the body which, when the liver is in harmony, brings us grace, flexibility and subtlety of movement. Signs of strong liver energy can be found in individuals who enjoy getting up early, are enthusiastic, energetic and humorous.

SUPPORT

A lifestyle that is spontaneous, free and active supports the Wood/Tree element. Stagnant, monotonous and pressurised lifestyles with little possibility for expressing new ideas potentially stagnates the liver. The liver also enjoys strong physical exercise as this draws on the supply of glycogen held within the liver and also brings flexibility to the joints, muscles and tendons. Early morning exercise prior to eating is beneficial for the liver. Shouting, singing and dancing all help release any tension that may have built up. Late night eating or overeating in general all dampen the spring-like quality that the liver represents. Having a traditional 'spring clean' is not only beneficial from a Feng Shui perspective but it also can rub off on the chi of your liver, especially if you practise a simple form of fast at the same time.

SELF ASSESSMENT

ORIENTAL DIAGNOSIS HAS BEEN practised by skilled practitioners for centuries and gives a holistic perspective on a client's current state of health. The beauty of the system is that it is not limited to one particular technique but encompasses several, and all of them are based on our senses. A skilled practitioner will observe posture, body language and facial expression, while at the same time enquiring about symptoms and at what time of day or night they appear the strongest. One important aspect of Oriental medicine is the part played by the network of channels, or 'meridians', that control the flow of chi energy around the body. The practitioner will be looking for imbalances in the meridians that may obstruct the flow of chi. These imbalances can be treated by applying pressure to special sites along the meridians known as acupressure points which, in turn, affect the function and health of the internal organs. Voice and expression can also reveal internal imbalances. Our habits, behaviour and cravings are all manifestations of some form of imbalance.

The use of Oriental Diagnosis in traditional healing is twofold. Firstly, it can be used to diagnose and form the basis of treating an acute problem. Secondly, a practitioner can detect the rumblings of a potential problem and devise a preventive course of treatment. There is initially what I call a mechanical level to this process in which various questions are asked and these, in turn, are assimilated by the practitioner so that a conclusion can be drawn. On another level, with skill and practice, this process becomes almost intuitive. The secret lies in the ability of practitioners to be totally 'empty' making their observations. They do not allow themselves to be filled with pre-conceived ideas, nor to be swayed too much by what the client thinks the problem is. On a basic level, all of us have intuitive diagnostic skills. If we haven't seen a friend for some time we notice immediately if he or she appears bright, alert, healthy or sad, distracted and unenthusiastic. It doesn't take any particular skill to do this; we can all perceive chi energy.

Although in this section I will relate diagnosis to looking at our current condition, the same 'way of seeing' can, with practice, be applied to our observations when looking at the home from a Feng Shui perspective. I am deeply grateful for the years I spent studying and practising this system before venturing into Feng Shui consultancy. Many of the same principles and practices apply to Feng Shui. You begin by seeing the 'big picture' and then narrow it down to the details. It is then easy to spot the major concerns you have that need to be emphasised and perhaps follow this up with several smaller points or details that need secondary attention.

The main benefit of seeing an Oriental medicine practitioner or an independent

Feng Shui consultant is that they have an objective view of you and your space. They can see the obvious while you are oblivious to it. For this reason, I have chosen a selection of Oriental diagnostic techniques which are easy to use and do not require a great deal of objectivity on your part.

How to use this section

As you work through the next nine sections related to acupressure points, facial diagnosis, emotions and so on, note if any of the statements relating to the Five Elements ring true with you at present. If you feel strongly that you can relate to the statement, then give the appropriate box a tick. For example, the acupressure point you press is the most painful, or the description of your habits or cravings really hits the nail on the head as far as you are concerned. Work your way through the various sections ticking boxes, and at the end of the exercise, note down which element is emphasised the most. It is not unusual for there to be imbalances in all the elements, however, one or perhaps two will show up the strongest. These are the Elements that you need to work on using the recommendations in the next chapter.

It is vital to remember that your condition is constantly changing. Therefore, the conclusion that you draw at the end of this section is only relative to who you are today. Please don't be left at the end of the assessment with the assumption that you have a lifelong Fire imbalance to contend with! As far as the recommendations are concerned in Chapter 7, they are best practised for 30 – 60 days to see a result and not a whole lifetime! Remember, everything changes!

Acupressure points

Always remember to use your thumb when you apply pressure to these points and breathe out as you press in. Press each of these points once and remember always to press the point on the opposite side of the body but never at the same time.

Water – Kidney

KIDNEY NO 1

This point is located on the sole of your foot, high up in the valley or crease you will find on the ball of your foot, below your toes. If you place the outside of your ankle on top of your opposite knee, and cup the top of your foot firmly, a small hollow will appear in the area of Kidney 1. Of all the acupressure points, this is the most difficult to activate and to feel any initial sensation. Most acupuncture points are on the surface of the body, but this one is very deep and needs more time and pressure until it 'wakes up'. Once you have located the point, a sharp pain is an indication of kidney stagnation.

Yes, sharp pain ☐   No pain ☐

WOOD/TREE – LIVER

LIVER NO 3
Find the webbing between your big toe and the adjoining second toe on the top part of your foot. Using your thumb, trace a path along the valley formed between the bones leading away from these two toes. High up in this valley, some two fingers' width above the webbing between the toes, you will find Liver No 3. A sharp pain when pressure is applied to this point is an indication of liver stagnation.

Yes, sharp pain ☐   No pain ☐

FIRE – HEART

HEART NO 7
Begin by tracing a line along the outside edge of your hand, from the little finger towards the wrist. When you get to the joint between the hand and the wrist, you will find a small depression or hollow in this gap. Flex your wrist a little bit to help you find Heart No 7. A sharp pain, discomfort, a tingling sensation or an 'electrical' sensation indicates stagnation with the heart.

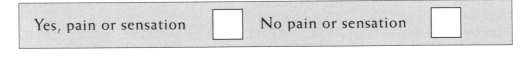

Yes, pain or sensation ☐   No pain or sensation ☐

Soil/Earth – Spleen/Pancreas

SPLEEN/PANCREAS NO 10

This point is found on the inside of the leg, just above the knee. Measure three fingers' width above the top of the kneecap and bring your other thumb into position on top of the bulge of muscle on the inside edge of the leg. A sharp pain here is an indication of stagnation in the spleen/pancreas.

Yes, sharp pain ☐   No pain ☐

Metal – Lung

LUNG NO 1

This point is found directly below the collarbone, between the first and second ribs. Begin by tracing the outline of your collarbone with your fingertips. Using a little more pressure, feel below the collarbone for the first and second ribs. Next, measure the distance mid way along the collarbone and then drop directly down from the collarbone with your thumb and Lung No 1 is between the first and second ribs. With your thumb in position, take a deep breath and apply fairly strong pressure as you breathe out. A sharp pain point at this point is an indication of lung stagnation.

Yes, sharp pain ☐   No pain ☐

FACIAL DIAGNOSIS

THIS FASCINATING ART can reveal much about your inherent constitution drawn from your parents and ancestors. Your bone structure and facial features are unchanging and, like your constitution, represent both your current nature and potential. In this section, I will concentrate on physical condition, which changes day by day and week by week. Using a large mirror in a well-lit environment, take a glance at your face. Try not to stare too hard for detail. Discoloration, puffiness, spots or prominent veins are all related to your current condition. The five primary areas of the face used for diagnosis are shown below.

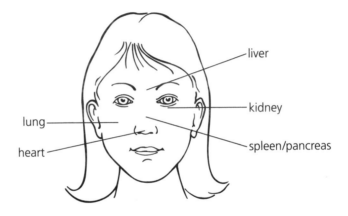

WATER – KIDNEYS

Potential kidney stagnation can be revealed in the area of the lower eyelid. Look out for signs of either a) puffiness, redness or swelling b) darkness – rather like a bruise.

a _____   b _____

WOOD/TREE – LIVER

Look in the area above the bridge of the nose, between the eyebrows. Check this area for (a) inflammation, discoloration, spots or dry skin. Deep lines in this area (b) can relate to previous liver imbalances and may not necessarily hold true today.

a _____   b _____

FIRE – HEART

Diagnostically, the heart is represented at the tip of the nose. Does this area appear either a) swollen, puffy, red or purple in comparison with the rest of your face or b) white and pinched like a knuckle on a clenched fist?

a ——————————   b ——————————

SOIL/EARTH – SPLEEN/PANCREAS

These organs are centrally located in the body and are represented in the centre of your face – the bridge of your nose. Check this area for either a) redness, yellow tinges, broken capillaries or b) a pinched and white appearance like a knuckle on a clenched fist.

a ——————————   b ——————————

METAL – LUNGS

The lungs are represented throughout the cheek area from below the cheekbone to a line between the corner of the mouth and the edge of the jaw. Check the area for a) redness, puffiness, broken capillaries, b) spots or c) pale, drawn almost grey skin.

a ——————————   b ——————————   c ——————————

EMOTIONS

THE OUTWARD EXPRESSION of your emotions, resulting from the ups and downs of daily life, provide an accurate reflection of the well-being of your internal organs. Here, we are looking at the more superficial expression of the emotions on a daily basis, rather than deep-seated emotional imbalances that could date back many years, even to childhood. Imagine if you gave your liver a 'hammering' one night by overeating, dining too late, drinking too much alcohol and not getting enough sleep. The next day you are likely to feel irritable, bad-tempered and impatient. It is this level of emotional experience that can vary within us all from day to day. The following questions are designed to measure your current emotional health.

WATER – KIDNEYS

Do you currently feel unusually anxious, fearful, worried or even paranoid?

Yes ☐   No ☐

WOOD/TREE – LIVER

Are you currently more irritable, impatient or angry?

Yes ☐   No ☐

FIRE – HEART

Are you currently excessively passionate or hysterical?

Yes ☐   No ☐

SOIL/EARTH – SPLEEN/PANCREAS

Are you currently complaining a great deal, feeling sorry for yourself, or are cynical or suspicious?

Yes ☐   No ☐

METAL – LUNGS

Are you currently more withdrawn, melancholic or depressed?

Yes ☐   No ☐

Habits

The external expression of your internal organs also affects how you go about our daily business. Unlike the emotions, these are expressions of your current way of being in the world. Have friends or colleagues recently criticised you for being too indecisive or erratic? Look around your home and notice if there are signs of incompletion, isolation or timidity which is protecting you from the outside world? See if any of these five areas really strike a cord with you at present.

Water

Are you currently less adventurous than usual? Are you being overly cautious or self-protective? Do you find yourself procrastinating and putting off making commitments?

Yes  No

Tree/Wood

Have others around you recently criticised you for being insensitive? Are you really listening and being sensitive to and aware of the needs of others? Are you being overbearing and domineering? Are you doing everything in a rush?

Yes  No

Fire

Does your life currently seem to be out of control? Are you dashing around in several directions at once, spinning wheels while apparently achieving little? Does your life seem out of control? Have others around you recently accused you of being self-centred? Are you erratic in your lifestyle – all action one moment and stillness the next?

Yes No

SOIL/EARTH

Are you becoming more dependent on others at the moment? Do you feel completely over burdened and that the situation is hopeless? The main area of concern here regarding your habits is incompletion. Do you have a list of unfinished projects, jobs, letters, conversations to have? Is there a current tendency in your life to leave things unfinished?

Yes ☐   No ☐

METAL

Are you becoming increasingly isolated in your life? Do you find it difficult to trust those around you? Are you becoming indecisive? Have you noticed that you have become more introverted lately? On a more chronic level, are you increasingly indifferent to the world outside of yourself?

Yes ☐   No ☐

CRAVINGS

THIS ASPECT OF ORIENTAL Diagnosis can seem paradoxical. Sometimes we crave tastes, flavours and sensations that can support a weak element while at other times, the craving is completely opposite – we cannot bear to taste at all. If any of these more extreme attributes ring true, then it shows an imbalance in an element. Looking through these five sections, try to notice what you are currently drawn to or violently disagree with.

WATER

Are you attracted to a lot of liquid at present? Do you prefer your food cold? Do you prefer savoury food or add extra salt or soya sauce to your meal? Do you absolutely dislike salt and never use any, even in your cooking?

Yes, I crave salt ☐   No, I hate salt ☐

WOOD/TREE

Do you currently crave food of a spicy nature? In particular, are you drawn to curry, Thai or spicy Chinese cooking at present? Do you crave sharp-tasting pickles, lemon or vinegar? Do you absolutely detest any or all of the above?

Yes, I crave spicy food ☐   No, I hate spicy food ☐

FIRE

Are you finding yourself drawn towards bitter-tasting food at present? Black coffee? Chocolate? Burnt toast? Do you dislike bitter-tasting greens like kale, spring greens or chard?

Yes, I crave bitter food ☐   No, I dislike bitter food ☐

SOIL/EARTH

Are you currently craving sweet, creamy, comforting foods? Are you attracted to sweet-tasting dairy products? Do you have a sweet tooth? Are your cravings self-indulgent?

Yes, I crave sweet food ☐   No, I hate sweet food ☐

METAL

Are you drawn towards dry foods – biscuits, toast, crackers? Do you prefer your food to be very well cooked – roasts, bakes and casseroles? Are you drawn towards strong condiments at present, such as a) pepper b) mustard c) horseradish? Do you have occasional cravings for strong, spicy food like a curry?

Yes, I strongly crave these foods ☐   No, I hate these foods ☐

TIME OF DAY

IN CHINESE MEDICINE, the five major organs and their complementary partners have a particular time of day when they re-charge and re-vitalise themselves. This is often the best time to introduce some form of remedy. From a diagnostic point of view, however, it can be very revealing if you consistently feel tired at this time or that symptomatic aches and pains are at their worst. Paradoxically, these can also be the times of day when we have unusual or erratic bursts of energy.

WATER – MIDNIGHT – 6 AM

Are you restless between these hours? Are any current symptoms worse between these hours? Do you have difficulty sleeping? Are you a night person?

Yes ☐   No ☐

WOOD – 6–10 AM

Are you at your worst in the morning? Do you dislike having to get up? Do you not begin to function until after 10 am? Do you always wake up early and are unable to go back to sleep?

Yes ☐   No ☐

FIRE – 10 AM– 2 PM

Are you at a low ebb at this time? Do you feel over-burdened or uninspired between these hours? Do you lack the enthusiasm that others around you may have at this time of day? Do symptoms generally recur between these hours?

Yes ☐   No ☐

SOIL/EARTH – 2– 6 PM

Do you lose your inspiration at this time of day? Do you feel tired? Do you need a siesta? Do you need to lift your energy with something sweet? Do general symptoms persistently recur during these hours?

Yes ☐   No ☐

METAL – 6 PM – MIDNIGHT

Is this your worst time of day? Do you feel withdrawn, isolated and anti social at this time? Are you always tired between these hours? Do you always eat late – close to midnight?

Yes ☐   No ☐

PHYSICAL EXPRESSION

YOUR BODY LANGUAGE and how you move is also an expression of your internal organs. It is a lot easier to see this in others and you may need to practise this while commuting to work or in a meeting until you become a little more aware of it.

With this new found awareness, it is easy to then notice how you are sitting, how you walk and how you express yourself physically – even in conversation.

WATER

Are you overly protective in your body language? Do you have a tendency to cross your legs? Do you fold your arms across your lower belly? Do you have a natural tendency to 'protect' yourself when in a room by a) positioning your back near the wall or b) positioning yourself so that you can always see the door?

Yes ☐   No ☐

WOOD/TREE

Do you always walk fast? Is there a certain stiffness to your gait? Are your movements jerky? Do you tend to clench your teeth or jaw?

Yes ☐   No ☐

FIRE

Are you very animated in your expression? Do you constantly gesticulate with your hands and arms? Is most of your physical expression coming from your upper body – your head and your hands? Are you constantly restless?

Yes ☐   No ☐

SOIL/EARTH

Do you tend to slump in your chair? Is your physical movement slow and ponderous? Do you carry an air of hopelessness? Do you cross your arms tightly around your midriff? Do you gesticulate vaguely with your hands and wrists allowing them to drop into your lap towards the end of the point you are making?

Yes ☐   No ☐

METAL

The extreme physical expression of a Metal imbalance is the lack of any movement. Do you keep very still? Do your shoulders stoop forward? Do you tend to curl up in a ball? Are you uncomfortable around others who gesticulate and express themselves wildly? Do you feel that you are in a shell?

Yes ☐   No ☐

VOICE

OUR VOCAL EXPRESSION changes from hour to hour and from day to day and is directly correlated to the health of the internal organs. Any obvious quality in the five examples set out below indicates an elemental imbalance. It is difficult to listen to your own voice, so you may need to tape record your voice and play it back. Again, as with the previous category, it would be wise to listen to those around you to get some practice in identifying the different 'voices'.

WATER

Does your voice sound wet, damp, weak? Does it sound like you are on the edge of tears, almost weeping?

Yes ☐   No ☐

WOOD/TREE

Is your voice sharp, loud and clear? Does it sound like you are shouting or arguing?

Yes ☐   No ☐

FIRE

Is your vocal expression erratic – this can be expressed as a voice that goes up and down or sentences that begin, stop, then begin. Does your voice sound like you are singing?

Yes ☐   No ☐

SOIL/EARTH

Is there a sense of incompletion in your vocal expression? This can be expressed by making a point and then meandering off the point. The syncopation can always be noticed in each sentence. You begin clearly and then your voice trails off. This expression is rather like sighing.

Yes ☐   No ☐

METAL

Is your voice rather dry and monotonous? Is there very little intonation in your speech? Is there an underlying presence of 'groaning'?

Yes ☐   No ☐

OBSESSIONS

ALTHOUGH THESE ARE extreme examples of various behavioural modes, they can be linked with your current condition. Here, as with all the other previous examples, see if you identify with any.

WATER

Are you obsessive about secrecy? Are you obsessed with sex? Are you sexually inhibited?

Yes ☐   No ☐

WOOD/TREE

Are you fanatical about exercise? Are you obsessed by order, ritual or time keeping?

Yes ☐   No ☐

FIRE

Are you excessively self-indulgent? Are you obsessed by your appearance – whether physical or style? Do you have a tendency to judge others purely on their appearance and the first impression they create?

Yes ☐   No ☐

SOIL

Are you obsessed by food? Do you always need to be in control? Are you prone to jealousy?

Yes ☐   No ☐

METAL

Are you obsessed by details? Are you obsessed by cleanliness and hygiene? Are you particularly possessive – either in relationships or in guarding your own property?

Yes ☐   No ☐

SYMPTOMS

THE FOLLOWING LIST of symptoms are very general, but they are useful in relating their overall expression to one of the Five Elements. Again, as with the other categories, only tick one if it is currently relevant.

WATER

Are you currently very tired? Do you have persistent lower back ache or pain? Do you have pain or swelling in your feet or ankles? Do you have a tendency toward ear problems?

Yes ☐   No ☐

TREE/WOOD

Do you have persistent eye problems? Do you feel stiff? Do your muscles give you pain, even after moderate amounts of exercise? Do you have general joint problems, especially the elbows and the knees?

Yes ☐   No ☐

FIRE

Are you constantly restless? Do you feel the cold? Are your hands and feet particularly cold? Do you have stiff inflexible fingers?

Yes ☐   No ☐

SOIL/EARTH

Are your muscles generally flaccid? Do you have a tendency to put on weight? Is there a lack of muscle tone on the inside of your thighs? Do you tend to accumulate weight around the hips and the buttocks?

Yes ☐   No ☐

METAL

Do you have a sensitive digestive system? Do chills and colds generally go to your chest? Are your wrists loose or flaccid? Are your forearms and upper arms generally weak?

Yes ☐   No ☐

CONCLUSION

RUN THROUGH THE various boxes that you may have ticked off and conclude which element or elements you need to pay attention to. Do remember that this is only who you are now and may not be representative of you in the future or indeed who you were in the past. Your condition is constantly changing. It is also helpful initially to focus on one or two elements only and work on these before addressing other problems. Positive ideas on how to bring about internal change will be covered in the next chapter.

Chapter Eight

Strengthening the Elements

I HAVE PREVIOUSLY EXPLAINED how to determine which element or elements are weaker in terms of your health and well-being. The purpose of this chapter is to explain the many facets of your life within which you could begin to bring about change. Working with the Five Element theory, it is important to:

1. Give the weakest element some support from any of the aspects that relate to it as listed in the sections to follow

and

2. Incorporate aspects from the preceding element on the cycle to give additional support.

I also recommend that you practise these changes to your lifestyle for at least 30 days and monitor the changes. There are many areas in which you can make changes including Feng Shui, food, exercise, music, relationships, holidays and entertainment.

Working on these areas of your life really reinforces your inner Feng Shui. I believe the essence of good Feng Shui is to balance our inner and outer worlds. Just a reminder: your inner Feng Shui represents your health and your chi while the outside influences are those based on your astrology

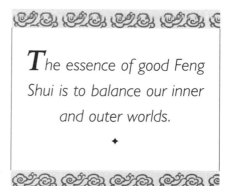

The essence of good Feng Shui is to balance our inner and outer worlds.

◆

(fate/destiny) and, of course, your living space. Remember, the elements you will need to strengthen will change as your emotions, life experiences and health go through changes.

CREATIVE QUALITIES OF THE FIVE ELEMENTS

HERE IS A REMINDER of the essence and characteristics of the Five Elements in terms of spiritual and emotional behaviour.

WATER
Courageous, curious, profound, adventurous, uninhibited, inventive.

TREE/WOOD
Energetic, flexible, spontaneous, creative, thoughtful, patient, sensitive.

FIRE
Calm, adaptable, friendly, warm, peaceful, social, outgoing, charming, inspiring.

SOIL/EARTH
Helpful, understanding, resourceful, sympathetic, passionate, reliable, steady.

METAL
Focused, dependable, detailed, stable, logical, insightful, humorous, positive, practical.

FENG SHUI

IN THIS SECTION I shall describe some of the supportive qualities of each of the elements that you could bring into your home. These will involve colour, style, lighting, imagery and Feng Shui remedies. You can use these recommendations in two ways.

Identify which element you are currently trying to strengthen in terms of your health and try the remedies listed here or emphasise their presence for a period of 10 – 30 days.

Refer back to this section for more detail when you work more specifically in Chapter 9 on your Life Aspirations.

WATER

To emphasise this element into your home, you need to think along the lines of water's gentle, meandering, calming, still, deep yin nature. Try the following ideas in your home.

COLOUR Black, deep blue.

STYLE The layout is ideally smooth flowing, meandering. Avoid any symmetry. Furniture design with plenty of curves and rounded edges.

LIGHTING Dimmer switches, water lights with dark or blue bases.

IMAGERY Images that invoke the spirit of contemplation, stillness and any water-related subjects.

REMEDIES Some form of water feature – fish tank, goldfish bowl, fountain.

WOOD/TREE

To emphasise this element think in terms of freshness, light, activity and new approaches.

COLOUR Greens, light blues.

STYLE Uplifting, bright, contemporary, fresh.

LIGHTING Uplighters.

IMAGERY Drawings, paintings, photographs, posters that evoke action and movement.

REMEDIES Plants.

FIRE

To strengthen this element you need to focus on warmth, colour, the unexpected and the vibrant.

COLOUR Reds, purples, lavenders, violets, pinks and sky blue.

STYLE Warm, comfortable, unconventional.

LIGHTING Candles, active magmalights, especially with red, purple or pink bases or interiors.

IMAGERY Paintings or posters that are colourful and modern. Images that portray passionate emotions.

REMEDIES Candles, fireplace.

SOIL/EARTH

To strengthen this element the overriding quality that you need to focus on is that of stability. You need to create a feeling of security and 'grounded' energy.

COLOUR Browns, yellows, oranges and ash grey.

STYLE Clutter free, open-plan layout. Square-shaped rooms or square-shaped layouts of furniture.

LIGHTING Table lamps – especially with low, squat bases, preferably gold, orange, yellow or brown colours.

IMAGERY Landscapes, mountains.

REMEDIES Natural crystals, clay vases, ceramics, clay figurines.

METAL

To bring a strong presence of metal into your home, your space needs to be orderly, functional, minimalistic and modern in design and layout.

COLOUR Whites, silver, dark shades of grey and gold.

STYLE Functional, smooth edges and surfaces. Practical and simple.

LIGHTING Spotlights.

IMAGERY Any art work that involves plenty of detail.

REMEDIES Hollow metal wind chimes, bronze figurines and coins.

FOOD

OUR INTERNAL FENG SHUI – our chi and our blood – is fed by our daily food. It is not merely our food's chemical composition that is important but its chi. By identifying the element that you wish to strengthen, work through the relevant section taking care to:

+ avoid or minimise the foods that can damage the element

+ emphasise the cooking style for the element *and*

+ work with some of the ingredients and tastes that are also listed.

This is only an overview of a fascinating subject but at least these minor adjustments have the potential to bring about a greater awareness of the chi of food.

WATER

DAMAGING Reduce your intake of cold foods, ice cold liquids, tropical fruits and ice cream.

COOKING STYLES Emphasise the warming quality that casserole-style cooking provides.

INGREDIENTS **Grains:** buckwheat, soba noodles. **Vegetables:** emphasise the use of seasonal root vegetables. **Fish:** shellfish including oyster, clams, mussels and lobster.
Taste/flavouring: salty/sea salt, naturally fermented soya sauce.

TREE/WOOD

DAMAGING Reduce the use of oil, fatty foods, deep-fried foods and alcohol.

COOKING STYLES Short term steaming or boiling with the lid off. Pickling and marinating.

INGREDIENTS **Grain:** wheat, oats, rye. **Vegetables:** leeks, spring onions, chives.
Fish: coastal fish including cod, haddock, halibut and herring.
Taste/flavouring: sour/pickles, vinegar and sauerkraut.

FIRE

DAMAGING Avoid excess use of salt. Reduce your intake of eggs including hidden eggs – cakes, pastries, pies and cookies.

COOKING STYLES Deep frying, wok frying, stir frying – all cooking with a high flame.

INGREDIENTS **Grain**: corn/maize. **Vegetables**: spring greens, chard, spinach. **Fish**: active ocean going fish – squid, octopus, eel and salmon.
Taste/flavouring: bitter/olives, roasted seeds.

SOIL/EARTH

DAMAGING Reduce or minimise the use of sugar and dairy foods. The worst combination would be baked flour products which include dairy and sugar such as cheesecake.

COOKING STYLES Use a low flame. Bring out the sweetness in the food with gentle sauté techniques.

INGREDIENTS **Grain**: millet. **Vegetables**: pumpkin, onions, cabbages and broccoli. **Fish**: freshwater fish including trout, carp and perch.
Taste/flavouring: sweet/jams, fruits, preserves and chestnuts.

METAL

DAMAGING Reduce or avoid all foods which are overcooked or burnt including toast and crackers. Reduce all animal fat.

COOKING STYLES Baking and roasting, steaming and boiling with the lid on for a longer period of time.

INGREDIENTS **Grain**: rice – preferably brown rice. **Vegetables**: watercress, kale, dandelion leaves. **Fish**: compact and active fish including sardines, whitebait and sprats.
Taste/condiment: spicy. Ginger and mustard.

LIQUID

GIVEN THAT WE ARE made up of some 60 per cent fluid, then the quality and quantity of our liquid intake is vital for our inner well being. The following guidelines will show you the types of fluids to drink according to which element you wish to strengthen.

WATER Avoid using ice, or taking in too much liquid. Focus on hot drinks. Drinks made from roots, especially dandelion root are beneficial.

WOOD/TREE Effervescent liquids are fine, sour or sharp drinks are excellent. Lemon juice or a slice of lemon in water is perfect.

FIRE Drinks need to be warming. Hot drinks that have a bitter flavour are ideal — many grain and root coffee substitutes are ideal.

SOIL/EARTH Ideally drinks need to be warm and sweet. Herb teas sweetened with barley malt or honey are beneficial. Hot, fresh apple juice is perfect.

METAL Try to avoid ice cold fruit juices and cold soy milk. Bring the pungent taste of ginger into your drinks. Ideally this is from the juice of raw, fresh ginger and not dried ginger powder.

EXERCISE

EXERCISE IS VITAL for increasing the oxygen supply to the blood, lungs and brain. It also speeds up your metabolism, which in turn allows the elimination and discharge process to be activated more quickly. Each of the elements can be strengthened by different approaches to exercise.

WATER Leisurely exercise — swimming is perfect. Exercise on water, such as rowing is also beneficial.

WOOD/TREE Here you will benefit from exercise that brings you greater flexibility, strengthens your reflexes and concentrates on the upper body. This could include any form of racquet sport.

FIRE Any exercise that is warming, vigorous and socially interactive — such as team sports.

SOIL/EARTH Exercise here needs to be grounding and incorporates being on the ground – such as walking, rambling or jogging.

METAL To strengthen this element, you need to develop your focus and concentration, and to open up the lungs and strengthen the belly, for example, by playing golf or cycling.

HOLIDAYS

WE ALL NEED TO TAKE a holiday to recharge and revitalise our chi. However, before planning your next holiday, think about which element you currently need to give support to and strengthen. Here are a few ideas to help you plan a holiday with a difference.

WATER This needs to be a holiday that is deeply relaxing – this could include an environment that is hot, by the sea and where you will be pampered! On the other hand, the Water element can be supported by stillness and some form of a retreat. It would be therapeutic, therefore, to either visit a health spa or plan a holiday that provides you with spiritual and emotional awareness, such as a retreat or a residential psychotherapy course.

WOOD/TREE Here you need to have a very active and physical holiday. Design a break that is challenging and energetic, such as sailing, hiking, trekking or exploring.

FIRE You will want to bring out your Fire aspect through activity, fun and socialising. Having a holiday with friends and colleagues that combines both the physical challenge with plenty of social life is ideal. Skiing would be a good example.

SOIL/EARTH Here you need a grounded, slower pace holiday. A traditional family holiday that is sociable, self-catering and more likely in a rural environment would support the soil/earth element. Ideally, this should be a holiday where everyone's needs are accommodated.

METAL This needs to be holiday that is both practical and educational. Metal is about focus and detail. This can be interpreted as a sightseeing or educational holiday. For someone else, this could be a holiday where you are alone or isolated. On the other hand, it could be one that is relatively active in a colder climate.

ENTERTAINMENT

EVEN THE KIND OF entertainment we are drawn to has its own particular form of chi. Drawn from the many possibilities that exist for us to choose from, here are examples based on the Five Elements. The kind of chi that we experience from these forms of entertainment has the potential to enhance, uplift and stimulate the element involved.

WATER Sedentary forms of entertainment where you are being entertained fall into this category. Darker, quieter environments also nurture the element of Water. The cinema would be a good example, especially if the film was either romantic or science fiction/futuristic. Watching a full day's cricket in a quiet, English village is the epitome of Water entertainment!

WOOD/TREE Here, the entertainment needs to be energising, involving and even vocal. Remember that the best release for liver/gall-bladder energy is expressing your energy through shouting. Watching soccer, rugby or any team event which involves cheering or yelling is ideal. Releasing pent up emotions through laughter is also ideal, therefore enjoying a comedy at the theatre or the movies is ideal.

FIRE Entertainment which releases and expresses our passion is beneficial here. The rollercoaster of emotions experienced through opera mirrors the energy of Fire and of the heart. Physical entertainment that involves being with others, such as dancing or nightclubbing, is also ideal.

SOIL/EARTH The grounded, warm and compassionate nature of Earth needs to be supported by socialising. Any entertainment that is centred around being with other people in a social atmosphere, especially if food is involved, is suitable. Dining out, entertaining others at home is perfect.

METAL This element symbolises focus and concentration and from an entertainment perspective, this could include activities that require your attention and solitude. Examples could include watching television, communicating through the Internet or as far as spectator sports are concerned, those that require focus, such as horse racing and motor racing.

COMMUNICATION

THE KIND OF RELATIONSHIPS that we are attracted to or get involved in have the potential to strengthen or weaken any of the Five Elements. Below, I describe the positive attributes of each element that you can build into communication with those around you during the 30-day period.

WATER Water is best expressed through profound, deep and intimate communication with others. There is often initial caution followed by a slow and steady approach to relationships.

WOOD/TREE The rising energy of dawn and spring expresses itself through a more independent and free-spirited approach to relationships. Communication is usually spontaneous, energetic and lively.

FIRE Fire is expressed through an outgoing, sociable and fun approach to relationships. Expressing passionately how you feel about someone is the epitome of the Fire nature.

SOIL/EARTH Encouraging relationships that are supportive, nurturing and caring describes this element best of all. Expressing your compassion, warmth and especially your listening skills is ideal.

METAL Relating to others on a more intellectual level that is clear, intense and focused, manifests the real nature of Metal. In addition to these qualities, commitment and reliability are positive attributes.

CLIMATES

CHOOSING A CLIMATE or particular prevalent weather conditions to support one of your elements can be extremely beneficial. Giving consideration to the element you want to strengthen when taking a holiday or a short break or even a major move for a new career abroad can have a very positive result.

WATER Cold climate.

WOOD/TREE Windy/fresh.

FIRE Hot.

SOIL/EARTH Humid.

METAL Dry – arid.

CLOTHING

WHAT WE CHOOSE TO wear on a daily basis is often drawn intuitively from how we 'feel' when we wake up. Ideally, it would be wonderful to have an enormous choice in our wardrobe to uplift and reflect the element we wish to strengthen that particular day. Here are some ideas based on style and colour that can enhance your element on a daily basis. Notice what you are particularly drawn to at present – does this reflect an intuitive re-balancing or are you simply attracted to colours and styles which reflect the current imbalance?

WATER Dark colours, especially black and navy support this element. Clothing that is loose, casual and flowing and also warm is ideal. Remember that many of the acupuncture points associated with the kidneys and bladder are in the region of your feet and ankles and any footwear needs to keep these areas protected and warm.

WOOD/TREE All shades of green and light blue can uplift the Wood energy. Vertical stripes, bright colours, and cotton clothing which is fresh and crisp are perfect. Wood energy is symbolic of the dawn, the spring and new beginnings – therefore anything which is currently in vogue is ideal.

FIRE Any shades of red including purples, mauves, violet, orange and pink are perfect, even if these colours are used only in moderation – such as in a tie or scarf or item of jewellery. Fire style is usually ostentatious and flamboyant. Whatever you wear it should get you noticed!

SOIL/EARTH Colours here are ideally creams and all shades of yellow including gold. Ideally, the style is comfortable, practical and earthy. Woollen, velvet, corduroy, boncle and home made garments and horizontal stripes also fit the bill.

METAL Colours here vary from white to shades of grey. The style is always conservative, formal, clean, clear and tidy. Metal is expressed by crispness, sharp lines and detail and smooth, shiney fabrics such as satin or silk. Business suits and formal evening wear fall into this category.

THERAPY

THERAPIES CAN BE powerful tools for self-discovery and each one, in a generalised way, can be associated with one of the Five Elements. If you are currently in some form of therapy or considering it, then from an objective perspective, notice which element is being expressed through that particular approach.

WATER All forms of vibrational healing, path healing and Reiki are intrinsically Water in their nature. Therapies that deal with our past, including re-birthing and past life regression are also Water.

WOOD/TREE Here, an energetic therapy is most helpful. From my own experience, a good example is Bio-energetics where the Wood element is stimulated through a series of physical exercises within a group, combined with space to verbalise the emotions in a spontaneous manner.

FIRE Therapy which involves working with a much larger group, such as psychotherapy in a group encounter situation, is primarily Fire by nature. Remember that the essence of Fire is its full outward expression followed by periods of stillness building up to the full Fire expression once more.

SOIL/EARTH Nurturing body work therapy often falls into this category, with examples such as shiatsu, reflexology and aromatherapy.

METAL The discipline and detail of acupuncture is obviously Metal by nature. The intensity and depth of hypnotherapy and one to one psychotherapy is focused and intense, mirroring the quality of Metal.

ESSENTIAL OILS

THE USE OF SCENT and fragrance has been present in many cultures for centuries. Without a doubt, this is our most primitive level of sensory perception and the subtle effects of essential oils can penetrate the most primitive level of our consciousness situated in the limbic brain. The fragrance from essential oils can gently penetrate the psyche and uplift our chi.

You will need an oil burner. Add 5–15 drops of any of these recommended oils to spring water and place in the container. Put a candle underneath and position the oil burner in the centre of the room. These oils can also be used effectively in the bath, or diluted in a suitable carrier oil and applied in a massage.

WATER Thyme, jasmine, sandalwood.

WOOD/TREE Grapefruit, camomile, lavender.

FIRE Rosemary, ylang ylang, tea tree.

SOIL/EARTH Fennel, frankincense, lemon.

METAL Eucalyptus, pine, cypress.

MERIDIAN STRETCHES

THE FOLLOWING SERIES of exercises are designed to stretch your body in a particular manner so that the meridians or energy lines in your body which are supported by each individual element get a good stretch. It would not be unusual for you to notice that the element that you need to work on may provide you with the most challenge. Try to persevere and always breathe out as you stretch. Relax the stretch and breathe in and then repeat the stretch 8–10 times. Notice how you feel over a 10–30 day period as a result.

WATER Sitting comfortably on the floor with your back straight and your legs together, reach forwards to touch the bottom of your toes or the soles of your feet or the insides of your ankles. As you breathe out, gently lean forward and pull yourself towards your ankles. Do not over stretch and simply take yourself to the limit. Notice where the tension is and always release with the out breath. Keep the backs of your legs straight and the ankles rigid with your toes pointing back towards your torso.

WOOD/TREE Sitting on the floor with your spine upright, open your legs as wide as possible. Bring some tension into the ankles by pointing the toes back toward your torso. As you breathe out, clasp your hands together and reach out towards your toes in one long, slow stretch. Breathe in, bring your arms back towards your torso and as you breathe out, stretch towards the opposite ankle and repeat the process.

FIRE Sitting on the floor with your spine straight, bring your knees up and place the soles of your feet together. Clasp your hands around the top of your feet and pull your heels in towards your groin. Take a deep breath and as you breathe out, stretch forward and try to bring your forehead towards your big toes. Relax and breathe in and repeat the exercise.

SOIL/EARTH For this exercise, you need to sit on your heels with your knees facing forwards. If possible, bring your heels either side of your buttocks. Stretch your arms above your head and slowly lean backwards until you can rest on your elbows. Provided there is not too much tension in your thighs or lower back, lower yourself gently to the floor and allow your arms to rest above your head. If you can manage this position for 2–3 minutes, it would be ideal, always breathing out and letting go of any tension. Initially, if this is difficult, then simply try sitting in the position and stretching upwards.

METAL Standing up with your spine straight, your legs straight and your feet and ankles together, reach behind your back with your hands and link your fingers together. Take a deep breath in and as you breathe out, bend forwards, keeping the backs of your legs straight while at the same time, raising your arms as high up as possible. Breathe in and return to an upright position. Repeat the exercise several times.

VISUALISATION

THIS IS A VERY POWERFUL tool to use to co-ordinate your mind, body and chi. First, find a quiet corner, and then begin by closing your eyes and paying attention to your breath. Only begin the visualisation process when you feel you are breathing from your 'belly'. In this undisturbed state of being, you could focus on any one of the five images below to support your particular element. I have used the general image of the different stages of a fruit tree in a seasonal cycle. Try to bring the image to your mind, allowing thoughts to come and go without any particular attachment to them.

WATER The imagery of seeds, of storage.

WOOD/TREE Visualise shoots, sprouting, emergence of new leaves.

FIRE Visualise the opening of buds, flowers and full blossom.

SOIL/EARTH Visualise the fruit and the kernel of the fruit.

METAL Focus on the falling leaves or the roots of the tree.

MUSIC

ON A SENSORY LEVEL, music certainly has the power to uplift us or we may use it simply to reinforce how we are feeling at any given time. Consider how often certain pieces of music have upset or annoyed you while at other times they seemed to fit the way you are feeling. What kind of music are you drawn to presently? Here are some ideas or styles of music that you could listen to, whether at home or in your car.

WATER Soul, reggae.

WOOD/TREE Classical music, string and wind instruments. Peruvian pipe music.

FIRE Jazz, opera.

SOIL/EARTH Country music, folk music, ballads.

METAL Military music, rock music, house music.

RECREATION

HERE ARE SOME GENERAL overviews of forms of recreation that can support each of the Five Elements. Recreation is a wonderful word – it literally means re-creation. In an ideal world, your choice of recreation can best be determined by what it would take to uplift or recharge your spirit. It is ideal to choose something that is totally different to your work. This means, for example, that if you spend your days at work embroiled in figures, detail and deadlines (metal), then your recreation needs to be some kind of activity that is opposite to this – not going home and spending time alone watching television or exploring the Internet for example!

WATER Recreation that is gentle, relaxing and deeply profound, such as meditation, aromatherapy or a long, hot bath.

WOOD/TREE Recreation which is energising, physical and spontaneous – any kind of sporting activity.

FIRE Recreation that is warming, stimulating and sociable. This could involve sport, parties or any kind of fun with a group.

SOIL/EARTH Recreation that is grounding. Usually this means activities which are home-based, that include gardening, sharing time with your family or completing any unfinished business.

METAL Recreation that involves accuracy, focus and detail – for many of us this means some form of study or research.

ACUPRESSURE

ACUPRESSURE IS EASY to use and you do not need a qualified practitioner to do the job for you. You are your own practitioner! Pressure is applied for 4–6 seconds. Always remember to breathe out as you apply the pressure, repeat it at least eight times and do not forget to work on the opposite hand, leg, finger or foot. It is best used upon waking, or at any time during the day when you have a moment's respite and at some time in the evening – but not just before you go to bed.

WATER Kidney Number 1 – located on the sole of each foot in the hollow or valley that is found below the ball of the foot. If you clench the top of your foot, you will form a natural hollow precisely where this point is located. It is one of the deepest points in acupressure and you need to apply a reasonable amount of pressure until you wake up the point.

WOOD/TREE Liver Number 1 – located on the inside of the big toe (adjacent to your second toe), find the spot where the nail joins the flesh. Press firmly and deeply into this area, either with your thumb or your thumbnail.

FIRE Heart Number 9 – this is found on the inside edge of your little finger (adjacent to your fourth finger) where the nail joins the flesh. Apply pressure here with your thumb or thumbnail from your opposite hand.

SOIL/EARTH Spleen/Pancreas Number 6 – this point is located on the inside of your leg, just above the ankle bone. Trace with your fingers along the inside of your shin bone from your ankle up towards your knee. Using your three middle fingers, measure a distance of three fingers above the ankle bone. Bring your thumb across and apply pressure above the three fingers.

METAL Large intestine Number 4 – this point is located in the fleshy valley between your forefinger and thumb. Bring the thumb of your opposite hand across, find the point and, as you breathe out, apply the pressure.

PART · FOUR

FENG SHUI
AND YOUR
HOME

Chapter Nine

Feng Shui and Chi

IN THE PRECEDING TWO SECTIONS, you have had the opportunity to put yourself on the map. Through unravelling who you are from an astrological perspective using 9-Star Ki, it is possible for you to determine:

1. Your character and potential

2. Where your chi is this year in terms of the Nine Houses

and finally

3. Which directions this year give you greater opportunity for success by working with the flow.

These are all vital components of any journey – whether real, intended or metaphoric. In Part 3 I showed you how to evaluate the state of your current chi – your physical condition. How is this manifesting in terms of your health and self-expression? What kinds of activities, dietary considerations and Feng Shui applications can strengthen and support your chi at present?

Having assessed your relationship with time using chi and the quality of your internal environment from a chi perspective, it is now time to check that your surroundings and home are also in harmony with your dream and journey at present.

In practice, whichever style or approach to Feng Shui you may have read about already, they all initially have one factor in common. Drawn from the traditional Form School of Feng Shui, they work with the obvious topographical features surrounding the home and consider how chi enters the home, circulates within the home and consequently supports the occupants. The Form School approach gives us the unique opportunity of studying the map of our environment – the topography, the layout and even how chi will affect the area at different times of the day and seasonally. Later, in Chapter 9, I will take you through aspects of Compass School Feng Shui where you will have the opportunity to apply more fine tuning. First, however, we need to familiarise ourselves with the territory.

Since Feng Shui is primarily concerned with perceiving our space from a chi or vibrational perspective, it is very subtle. However, it is also a very powerful and potent system and rather like various forms of vibrational healing, its effects can be long-lasting.

There is an interesting overlap between Feng Shui practice and energetic healing that is becoming more mainstream in modern society such as acupuncture, acupressure, Shiatsu, Chinese herbal medicine, homeopathy, reflexology, aromatherapy, Bach flower remedies and Reiki. For the optimum benefits from any of these systems, a practitioner will always recommend that patients take care of themselves in order to support the subtle changes that they are encouraging. Most practitioners will point out that over stimulating your body with the use of caffeine, chocolate, sugar and spicy food or sensitizing your body with excess dairy and animal products will simply slow down the potential for deeper and more subtle change.

This process is also mirrored in Feng Shui. Fine tuning of Feng Shui remedies is best achieved once you have dealt with the 'big picture' – balance the chi of the home and then the fine tuning can take place.

The importance of ensuring you have good soil in which to plant seeds is obvious. The first job for any farmer or gardener is to prepare the soil. Is it well composted? Is it alkaline enough? How moist is the soil?

From the same perspective, in this chapter, we can prepare your home for the aspects of Feng Shui fine tuning from Chapter 9 that will combine effectively with the work you have already done in terms of your own chi in Parts 2 and 3.

THE MAP OF THE TERRITORY

FOR THIS INITIAL exercise, as in any form of Oriental Diagnosis, you need to be as objective as possible and try to gain some distance from your living space to help you see potential problems more clearly. The best way to check the chi of your immediate environment and your community is to have a good walk through your neighbourhood, taking note of the following areas that you need to consider.

> *Chi is being generated and discharged by us constantly and over time, our immediate environment begins to absorb it.*
>
> ✦

STEP 1

From the widest possible perspective, consider what kind of chi your locality has. The quality of this chi will naturally attract certain types of home dwellers. Is the area quiet, secluded, secure and safe, or is it noisy, vibrant and frenetic? Does the area attract mainly students, young couples, families or the elderly? Are the homes occupied mainly by people who are stable and have lived there for generations or does the area attract people who are on short leases? Whatever the level of chi or activity in your neighbourhood, it will undoubtedly affect you as well.

STEP 2

Next, it would be wise to check out the chi of your locality at different times of the day and at different times during the week. This is especially true if you are planning to buy or rent a new property. While you might be attracted by the chi of a neighbourhood one quiet sunny Sunday morning, you may be surprised to discover that the quiet leafy street you move into becomes a major thoroughfare of traffic on Monday morning! All of us generally take this into consideration in the first place before selecting a property – we have in mind an area or neighbourhood that we are attracted to for either geographical reasons or because we are already familiar with the area. Perhaps for many months or years we have dreamt that this is where we would like to relocate. It is often this visualisation and a clear idea of what we are looking for that leads to a successful outcome.

STEP 3

Again, from an objective perspective, notice where your home is located in relation to adjacent buildings. Does it appear to be hemmed in and overshadowed by neighbouring buildings? Does your home receive plenty of sunlight as this provides a natural charge of chi for the home and the occupants. From the Form School tradition, is there a real or symbolic hill or mountain behind the property to give you support and protection? In reality, this could be a building, a wall, a fence or a gentle upward slope away from your property.

STEP 4

Check what kind of buildings are in your immediate vicinity. Do you have a school or playground nearby? The chi of these buildings and spaces can be associated with powerful wood energy – growth, stamina, freshness and the spirit of spring. Do you live opposite a vacant site of land that is awaiting re-development? The rubbish, the stagnation of the site all has the potential to affect your chi in a more yin way. Is the road outside your property quiet or busy? All roads are symbolically associated with the movement of chi, in the same way that rivers have this association in traditional Feng Shui. Busy, noisy highways outside your home are yang forms of chi and can be very distracting. On the other hand, do you live in a quiet, cul de sac or a road that is a dead end? Although the chi will be quieter in such a location, it will obviously have the potential to stagnate – so how is this going to affect your health, career and journey at present?

Overall, in this initial stage in assessing the chi of your locality, I encourage you to rely on your 'gut feeling' – your intuition. Think about what attracted you to the area in the first place. Frequently, what we are attracted to in terms of chi is mirrored by our own chi at the time. Our chi and our condition can colour our intuition and we can be drawn to properties and locations that mirror our internal expression of chi.

THE HISTORICAL CHI OF YOUR HOME

THE HISTORY OF YOUR property has the potential to affect your chi and your own journey in two ways. Firstly, we can all be affected by the chi of the previous occupants and secondly, the shape, the design and the original use of the building – if it is a conversion – will undoubtedly affect our chi.

Perhaps you have walked into a friend's kitchen unexpectedly when, until you reached the door, they had been engaged in a violent argument. As you enter the room, everyone falls silent but you can cut the chi in the air with a knife! We call this energy vibration. On a more subtle level, chi is being generated and discharged by us constantly and over time, our immediate environment begins to absorb it. Our patterns of behaviour, our emotions, our routine all generate qualities of chi which are essentially yin and, with time, they will be absorbed by the more yang elements in our surroundings – the bricks, stone, timbers, mortar, plaster and of course the soft furnishings, such as carpets and curtains.

Find out what you can about the previous occupants of your space. Unbeknown to you, your journeys have become linked. Were they a young couple who had become successful, outgrown their space and moved on to a more expensive property? Were they a young family who had recently had another child and needed more space? Were they an elderly couple who had enjoyed good health in their twilight years? Had the previous occupants recently divorced or separated? Had the previous owner gone bankrupt or had the property been repossessed by the mortgage company? Obviously you want to pick up on the best elements of their journey and not be distracted by the potentially damaging quality of chi that is left behind.

In any situation, it is very wise to consider the validity of some form of space clearing ritual when you take up residence in a new space. Ideas on this practice are covered in Chapter 10. Essentially, it is about clearing the cobwebs of old chi and imprinting with clear intention your chi, your dream, your vision into the space. Space clearing is also effective when you are renting a fully furnished home or simply staying overnight in a hotel or motel. In a nutshell, it helps to purify the space and set the tone for your own chi which supports your journey.

THE 'GATE' OF CHI

IT IS IMPORTANT TO regard the home as a living, breathing organism. The main nutrient of our home is chi and the harmonious internal circulation of chi is vital for health and success in life. Metaphorically, the front door is the mouth of the home – through which the chi enters – and so you need to look carefully at the immediate surroundings to the door, both internal and external. The front door is where we make a transition from the internal to the external and vice versa. Not only can good or bad chi enter through the front door but new opportunities and new possibilities may enter as well. From a yin/yang perspective, our home represents many of the yin elements. It is somewhere to which we retreat, to rest, recharge and recreate our chi. We do not need a howling gale of chi roaring into our space and throwing us into confusion, while at the same time, we need more than a small trickle of chi which would give us limited potential.

As chi approaches your home, it bounces off aspects of the external environment, absorbing qualities from the immediate vicinity of the front door, before bringing them into the home. Since you spend a lot of time in your home in a vulnerable state, asleep, resting or eating, you need to feel a sense of security, which can be achieved by providing some protection at the front of the property. This can be in the form of a hedge, a fence, a gate, healthy shrubs or trees – preferably planted in odd rather than even numbers.

Next, you should keep the front garden, driveway and path clear of old, dead debris as aspects of this dead chi can also be brought into the home. It is good practice to clear up dead leaves and litter, trim back or remove dead plants and dead or dying trees. Avoid keeping your rubbish bin outside your front door and if you have a cat who is a voracious hunter, make sure it is not leaving dead birds and dead mice close to your front door!

Chi energy is rather like water in a river; its healthy expression is a meandering nature. Therefore, when you have a close look at your pathway from the front door to the road, try to avoid a design that is direct, straight and like an arrow aiming at your front door. A meandering path is ideal or, if this is not practical, try to place circular tubs of plants offset from each other on either side of the path to create a meandering effect. Sharp angles generate a quality of 'prickly' chi which is not inviting or comforting to you or your visitors as you enter the home.

Chi also has the potential to bounce off structures and this deflected energy becomes more focused and potent. The more dominant or sharper the structure, the more powerful the rebound of chi. Traditionally, this is known as 'cutting chi'. If there are structures within 100 feet (30 metres) of your front door that are deflecting cutting chi at the front door, you need to remedy it. Sources of cutting chi can include the edges of adjacent buildings where their 90 degree angles are pointing directly at your front door, a telegraph pole or a utility pole within 100 feet (30 metres) of your front door, the sharp edge of an adjacent roof eave aimed at your front door, a lamp-post or an unhealthy tree. To assess whether you have any of these sources of cutting chi, it is best to stand in the entrance way of your home and look out. The best known protective device in dealing with cutting chi is known as the Pakua mirror.

The Pakua mirror

Available from most Feng Shui stockists, the Pakua mirror is about 3 ins (7.5 cm) across and incorporates on the outer circle trigrams from the *I Ching* set out in the Earlier Heaven Sequence. At the centre, is a circular mirror which deflects cutting chi, thereby protecting your home. You can hang this device above or to the side of the door, preferably facing the source of cutting chi.

Chi is not always one-way traffic aimed at you. What can you do to the front of your property to give an 'impression' of protective chi, uplifting chi or healthy chi? For example, a beautifully kept, albeit small, front garden or radiant blossoms in window boxes will always attract the eye of a passer-by. It may uplift their chi and they will then look your property in a positive way. On the other hand, a front garden laden with debris, old bicycles and a skip that is the eyesore of the whole street, will encourage negative chi to be aimed at your front door by passers by!

For centuries the Chinese have placed statues of animals either side of the gates of homes and temples to represent protection or stability or longevity. Many home owners in the West place lions as symbolic guardians beside their front door, or owls or eagles to keep a watchful eye. On a subtle level, they represent and emanate the chi of protection.

There are also other ways to create a more 'uplifting' feeling of chi at the façade of the property and especially around the front door. In an ideal world, we would walk 'upwards' towards the front door. There might be a path sloping up towards the property, or a few steps we must walk up to reach the front door. Any numbers or a name of the property near the front door should also be positioned in such a manner that they slope up toward the right. For example, if the number of your property is 104, then the central zero would be at the centre of the plate, the one to the left, slightly lower, and the four to the right, slightly higher.

$$1 0^4$$

External lighting around the front door can also be more uplifting. Rather than no lighting at all, or lamps that hang downwards, look at positioning spotlights in the shrubbery near the front door at ground level to light up the porch. If this is impractical, consider a form of lighting close to the front door or in the porch that has an uplifting effect. If there is no outside light at all and the area is dark and unwelcoming, install one as soon as possible and keep it on until you are ready to sleep.

THE DOOR

IF YOU LIVE IN a block of flats, you need to consider the door to your apartment. You also need to pay some attention to the main communal door to the property as this is where chi enters the building initially. If you have two doors to your home, pay particular attention to the one you use most. In some approaches to Feng Shui, it is the door the architect designed that you would need to consider. However, chi is going to enter through the door that is used most often.

Obviously, the most protective form of door is a solid one so that you do not feel vulnerable as you recharge and recreate your chi during sleep and rest. If you plan to use glass within the door, it is better to have it in the higher sections only, rather than throughout the entire door. It is fine to have two doors adjacent to each other, provided they are of the same design – different styles, panelling or glass, creates a confusion of chi as it enters the home. Make sure that the whole area around the front door is clean and free of cobwebs, dead leaves and old newspapers. Check that the door is functioning properly – that it doesn't squeak or groan when you open it, that it is not stiff and awkward to open, or needs to be slammed to close it. Any malfunctions like this have a negative effect on you and they also give a sense of unease to your guests as they struggle to open the door. Make sure you are easy to find! Do you have a name plate, and a well-lit doorbell, and does the bell actually work? Finally, provide a good quality doormat for your guests. Throughout the world, different cultures encourage you to leave your shoes outside or in the hallway, ranging from Japanese homes, to Asian mosques and temples. The principle is simple. As you enter the more peaceful yin environment of the home, you leave outside the stagnant chi that you have picked up on your travels. Just as we would always consider washing our own towels frequently, as they pick up dirt and germs, be sure to replace your front doormat regularly, as it will not only absorb mud and debris but also plenty of dead chi.

HALLWAY

As CHI ENTERS YOUR home through the door, it needs to circulate freely within the space. Therefore, keep the area adjacent to the door and any hallway passage or corridor clear of obstructions and diversions. Notice how you feel when you enter a space that is warmly lit, welcoming and where you can see clearly where you are going. Compare this with being greeted by a dimly lit hallway that is cluttered with bicycles, boxes, suitcases and stacks of hiking boots! You can improve the quality of your own chi, and that of your guests when they enter your home, by placing some form of imagery on the wall adjacent to the door that catches your eye as you enter. Think of a piece of art that gives you a sense of calm, or is welcoming or inspiring. Not only does it uplift your spirit when you enter but it is also the last image you will take with you as you leave the home.

The Ideal Front Door Scenario

✦ Ensure there is no view of the back door from the front door. In this situation, chi will enter through the front door and rush through the home like a gale and disappear out through the back door. During this process, it is unlikely to charge the adjacent rooms and it is symbolic of losing opportunities in terms of your external activities – your career, your work and your relationships with neighbours, family and friends. To slow the flow of this chi, place metal or wooden wind chimes in the hallway between the front door and the back door, well above your head. These have the effect of slowing down this rush of chi. You could also use a screen or curtain.

✦ Ensure there is no view of the toilet from the front door. Many homes have a toilet or cloakroom close to the front door. If this is the case, always keep the toilet door shut. To help make the door into a window place a 5 inch square mirror above eye level on the outside of the door.

✦ Ensure there is no view of the bedroom from the front door. Ideally, bedrooms should be sited as far away as possible from the busy chi that is found close to the front door. All of us feel more safe and secure when we can sleep as far as possible from any source of distraction or potential threat. Otherwise, the only immediate solution is to keep this door closed.

✦ Ensure there is no view of the kitchen from the front door. Worse still is the cooker being visible. On a subconscious level, if the first room that you see as you enter the home is the kitchen, you will always be thinking about food or eating. This can create a tendency to overeat and consequently lead to obesity. If there is space to fit a door, then consider a glass panelled one which protects the kitchen but at the same time allows light to enter. You could also consider hanging 'distracting' images that catch your eye as you walk through the hall. For example, paintings of landscapes or photographs of the family will divert your attention away from the kitchen and thoughts of food.

WINDOWS

ANOTHER OBVIOUS source of chi entering your home is through your windows and these ideally need to be kept clean so as not to filter the chi through grime and dirt as it enters your space. At the same time, very strong bright sunlight can have an overbearing effect on a room and you may need to use curtains, blinds, screens or shutters to diffuse any excessive glare. Windows also need to be proportional to the space. Too few windows, or windows that are relatively small, will obviously let in less light and less chi. Occupants of this kind of a home are going to feel more isolated, sedentary and retiring. On the other hand, windows that are huge in proportion to the space can bring too much chi into the home, which can have the effect of distracting or overcharging you. Occupants of this kind of a home will often feel restless, find it difficult to concentrate and have more desire to spend time

The Ideal Window Scenario

✦ Windows should be functional. Make sure that all your windows are in good repair, they open easily and are kept clean.

✦ Windows should open outwards. This reflects the aim of embracing the chi and the fresh air.

✦ Skylights should be correctly positioned. Although skylights offer practical solutions to tight spaces, there are some locations where they are not suitable. Avoid sleeping under a skylight – this encourages your chi to dissipate while you are asleep while at the same time, the powerful chi from the heavens can have an overbearing effect. Avoid placing the cooker under a skylight – this allows energy from your cooking to dissipate out through the skylight. It is rather like constantly cooking food without using a lid. It does not concentrate the chi. Avoid placing your desk under a skylight – this encourages your chi, ideas, inspiration and concentration to dissipate. If this is unavoidable, consider moving your desk slightly to one side of the skylight to avoid the distraction while at the same time, enjoying the light that it provides.

outside of the home, often spending their money. Modern architecture, with an emphasis on huge windows and glazed French doors, is symbolic of a culture of overspending and living on credit.

I recently checked out a local fast food outlet while researching the subject of chi in business locations. The chi was so bright it was almost overbearing. The lighting was extremely strong, the colours very bright and most of the walls were glazed from top to bottom. It created an ambience that was so highly charged that you did not feel you could linger for long – even the seating reminded me of a waiting room at a railway station. In contrast, you can enter a dimly lit restaurant with comfortable seating, soft music, quietly hospitable staff to wait on you and feel encouraged to stay for hours. These are two examples of how light and chi affect our mood.

YOUR BEDROOM

THIS IS YOUR ULTIMATE inner sanctum where you are at your most vulnerable while you sleep and recharge your chi. From a yin /yang perspective, this is a more yin, quiet and peaceful environment; you need to feel protected and do not want distracting and powerful chi to disturb you. At the same time, there needs to be a good circulation of chi and plenty of fresh air available to recharge you. Ideally, the bedroom should be as far away as possible from the front door, mirroring the practice of our prehistoric ancestors who did not sleep in the mouth of their cave!

Naturally, the most important item of furniture here is your bed and its position relative to the source of chi entering or exiting your room is vital for a good night's sleep. On entering your bedroom, note where the windows are located. Chi tends to travel between the door and any windows, so avoid positioning your bed in line with this 'draught' of chi. The next consideration is to position your bed so that you can see the door from where you sleep. This gives you a deep sense of inner security. If it is feasible, position your bed as far away from the door as possible. Finally, avoid sleeping with your head close to a window as your chi will dissipate through the window and make you feel more tired on awakening.

If you have a bathroom, toilet or shower leading off your bedroom, make sure that the toilet door is always shut while you are asleep. Check which side the door to your bedroom is hinged. The ideal situation is for your door to open out freely

> *Your bedroom is your inner sanctum where you are at your most vulnerable while you sleep and recharge your chi.*
>
> ♦

into the room. In some Edwardian or Victorian homes it was fashionable to hinge a door the opposite way so that, on entering, you were greeted by a blank wall. This was to give you extra privacy while you slept, changed or washed. In this situation, however, you are potentially reducing the flow of chi into the room.

To help you protect your own chi while you are asleep, to internalise it and recharge it, make sure you have a strong, stable headboard. Chi energy enters and exits the body through the feet, hands and the top of the skull. Having a solid 'mountain' behind you while you sleep is far more beneficial than a cold, blank wall or worse, the cutting chi of an ornate brass bedstead.

Note the position of your bed relative to the wall that it is up against. Is it equidistant – in the middle of the wall? This is vital in a relationship as it gives both individuals who share the bed equality in the relationship. A shared bed crammed into the corner of a room, is giving more freedom of chi to the individual on the open side whereas the partner will literally and symbolically feel up against a wall. For added stability and protection in the relationship, you can place matched bedside tables on either side making sure that all edges are rounded to prevent cutting chi being focused towards the occupants.

Ceiling beams above the bed are a Feng Shui nightmare! Not only can they be a source of cutting chi but as the beams are supporting the roof or floor above you they carry a tremendous load, and this pressure is focused into the beams generating chi which continues downwards, placing direct pressure on you while you sleep. There are a number of solutions to this scenario including:

1. Painting the beams to make them 'disappear',

2. Hanging two Chinese bamboo flutes 2–3 in (5–7.5 cm) below the beam to soften the load – bamboo is hollow, light and yin to counterbalance the beam (the flutes are hung at a 45 degree angle to the beam with the mouthpiece downwards),

3. Building a false ceiling,

4. Pinning muslin, a drape or linen across the beams,

5. If you live in a period property where beams are one of the finest features of your home, consider getting a four-poster bed. This is in keeping with the style of the home and will provide a canopy for your protection.

One of the most important qualities we look for in a long-term relationship is stability. Since the bed you share with your partner is symbolic of this relationship, it too needs to be stable. Beds that are rickety or likely to fall apart speak volumes about the state of the relationship! The mattress or futon that we lie on needs to be replaced, aired and cleaned frequently; remember that we spend up to a third of our lives here. All soft furnishings, such as curtains, carpets, bed linen and especially the mattress, absorb chi. Therefore, I would never consider buying a second-hand mattress. I would be wondering who had been using it before. Were they happy? Were they ill? Did they die in the bed? I wouldn't even want to know!

Given that the bedroom is a more yin environment, the lighting that you choose needs to reflect this. Soft lighting is ideal. Avoid having ceiling lamps directly over the bed as they could be a source of cutting chi. If you have a ceiling light in the centre of the room, which represents the balancing point of the space, make sure the shade is designed in such a way that it does not provide cutting chi. Overhead lamps that form into a sharp point below them are the worst type to have in any room – but especially a bedroom.

Colours should match the lighting and should be soft and warm. Pastel colours are better than bright white, bright red, deep black and so on. If you are fond of strong colours, incorporate them into the decor in the room in small amounts – a bright bedspread, a bright lampshade, a bright sash for the curtains or a brightly coloured stool or chair.

Mirrors can also pose a problem with regard to chi in the bedroom as they tend to stimulate the chi making it difficult to rest, relax and sleep. In times gone by, people either never possessed one or if they used them for dressing, they kept them in an adjacent room known as the 'dressing room'. In this day and age, they are often found in the bedroom. While very useful for protection or even enhancement, they also have the capacity to drain your chi while you are asleep. Avoid sleeping with your image visible in any mirror. The worst scenario of all is a mirror at the foot of your bed. Ideally, remove these mirrors or, if this is not possible, cover them up while you are asleep. If you need a full-length mirror for dressing, consider hanging it on the inside of a cupboard door.

As you lie in your bed, notice what is on the wall straight ahead of you when you wake up. Waking up to an image that inspires you can really set the tone for the day. Do you have a favourite painting, or a window with a wonderful view? Perhaps you wake up with a view of cluttered bookshelves, an untidy wardrobe or boxes and magazines that should be relegated to the municipal dump!

As we already know, not only is chi circulating in our space but we are also being charged by the two fundamental forces of Heaven and Earth. Having dealt with beams, lights or other obstructions above the bed, you also need to check if anything is potentially blocking the energy that you receive from Earth via the ceiling below you, through the floor and most importantly, the space between the carpet and your mattress. Try to keep this area completely clear and get rid of any unwanted items that might be lurking there.

A headboard is vital, as is making sure the bed is
positioned in the middle of the wall.

Given that the bedroom is primarily a yin environment for rest, you need to minimise the use of the electrical gadgets connected with your day to day 'busyness'. These might include a mobile phone and its charger, fax machine or a computer. At the very least, switch these off before you go to sleep, cover them up and, ideally, remove them from the room. Televisions, videos and even a bedside radio or digital clock emit electromagnetic frequencies that can disturb your sleep. The most powerful of all, the television, is best not kept in the bedroom but if you must have it there keep it at least 9 feet from your bed and make sure you turn it off before you go to sleep and take the plug out of the socket.

Finally, try out all these ideas, or some of them at least, for a minimum of 10 days to notice the benefits. There is very little value in trying this or that just for one night to see if it has any effect. In the same way, despite all the differing opinions regarding the best position of your bed, try out different ones until you find the one that seems satisfactory. Most of this is common sense, some of it is intuitive and certainly some of it is scientifically based. It is your space, so you need to make it work for you.

THE KITCHEN

IN MOST TRADITIONAL cultures, the kitchen is regarded as vital to the health and welfare of the family; it can even be regarded as sacred. In a similar spirit, our own mothers and grandmothers would severely reprimand us if we fooled around in their space, made their floor messy, tinkered with their cooking pots while they were preparing a meal or upset the contents of the fridge. The cook is responsible for nourishing the family, and this is where our blood and chi originates. In traditional Feng Shui, the kitchen was reasonably secluded and definitely off limits for pranksters and general traffic. Cooking is undoubtedly one of the highest expressions of love and cooks need a space where they can begin to create the health of the family in peace and quiet.

The kitchen therefore must have no 'through draught' of chi. An example of a through draught is where the front door faces the kitchen and the back door. The cook also needs to have a feeling of focus without distractions and therefore an ideal position for a cooker is away from the door. At the same time, it should be positioned so that the cook can actually see the door from where they are working, thus creating a sense of security. For practical purposes, if this is not possible, consider installing a mirror on the splashback behind the cooker, angled in such a way that the cook can see the door. Remember, chi energy not only enters through windows and doors but also dissipates. Try to avoid placing a cooker directly underneath a skylight or directly in front of a window – just to the side is perfect. Check the area where the cook usually stands for sources of potential cutting chi. Sharp edges from the kitchen table or other units within this space are obvious sources. Another potential source of cutting chi is the hood from the extractor unit which is often at head level or higher. Notice whether this is bearing down directly on you in any way.

> *I*n most traditional cultures, the kitchen is regarded as vital to the health and welfare of the family; it can even be regarded as sacred.
>
> ◆

Since the dawn of civilisation, we have cooked with fire and the recommended modern version of this flame is the use of gas rather than electricity or microwave cooking. While a flame will not necessarily change the nutritional value of the food compared to the use of electricity or microwave, it will certainly change the chi. I personally dislike the lack of visible control that electricity or microwave cooking provides me with as I cook. The flame is the full expression of fire energy and, as such, is a microcosm of what the source of so much of our chi in life is – the sun. Simply speaking, when we cook we are placing a little bit of sun under our food. With skill and practice, we can adjust this fire to suit our needs. If you have not cooked on a flame for a long time, consider preparing your food on a gas stove (even a portable camping unit) for a 10 day period and notice not only how different the food tastes but also the change of chi that you become aware of.

There is a strong possibility of a clash of elements within the kitchen – namely Fire and Water. In the diagram below you can see how important it is to separate the elements of Water and Fire. From a Feng Shui perspective, it is considered unwise to position water either opposite the cooker or adjacent to it. In this context, water means the sink but can also include the fridge, the deep freeze, the dishwasher or a washing machine. However, the first three are the most important. If this is unavoid-

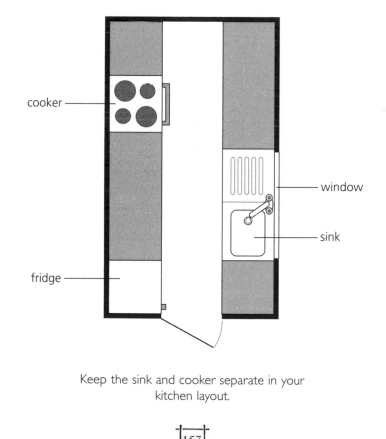

Keep the sink and cooker separate in your kitchen layout.

able, then the obvious solution is to re-site one of the elements or, if they are adjacent to one another and if this is impractical, place the mitigating element –Wood/Tree between the two features. This could be achieved by hanging a picture of a plant or placing a live plant between the two elements. You could also introduce the colour green into this area.

Keeping your cupboard, larder and fridge well stocked implies abundance, richness and even generosity. We can all recall the experience of chi when we open an empty cupboard or a poorly stocked refrigerator in search of something to eat! By having plenty of food in storage and even by cooking a little more than we need, we express the chi of hospitality and friendship. In the same way, serving stingy portions expresses the kind of chi that is too tight, too yang and lacks real warmth.

Central cooking stations in the middle of the room are becoming popular in modern kitchen design. From a chi perspective, this can work for some individuals and not for others. Some cooks prefer the focus and concentration of this kind of cooking whereas others would like to be at the centre of the room, involved in all the traffic and have the kind of chi that thrives on this situation. If you have such a feature or wish to design one, make sure that the edges are rounded to avoid cutting chi and remember the obvious conflict of Fire and Water.

Unlike in traditional times, the kitchen has now tended to become the focal point for eating. This makes sense as it is naturally one of the warmest rooms in the house and, with a little care, the position and layout of the dining area can bring great harmony and communication to the members of the household. Consider the effect of people eating on stools, with no mountain (support) behind them, at a kitchen bar-type table that faces a wall. It encourages hurried eating and little communication. On the other hand, a layout that includes a stable, preferably round, table surrounded by comfortable supportive dining chairs, ideally in even numbers, sets the tone for communication and focus. I personally really value sitting around the table and sharing a meal with my family. It is, for me, the highlight of the day. Communication is possible, sharing is possible, rather than individual members dashing off to their rooms with their plate or sitting in another room in front of the television completely out of communication. As with all areas of your home, if you set the tone using the essential understanding of chi in both the design and layout of space, you are simply supporting and stage-managing a healthy, vibrant environment.

DESK/WORK STATION

INCREASING NUMBERS OF people are beginning to either work from home or bring their work home from the office. Rather like the yang, structured discipline of an office environment, your desk and your work station at home needs to encourage this dynamic energy. On the other hand, you may be looking at this area of your home for your own studies or for your children's homework assignments. In all of these scenarios, there are fundamental Form School principles that you can apply to this vital area of your life.

The advice for your work area is rather like that for the bedroom where it is paramount that you position the bed to avoid lying in a draught of chi that can exist between the door and any windows. The first step, therefore, is to make sure that your work desk, or wherever you are sitting, is not in a direct line between the door and a window. Next, consider positioning your desk so that you can see the door clearly from where you sit. This gives you a far greater sense of security while you concentrate on your work. It is important for your concentration that you do not place your desk directly in front of a window, especially if it has a beautifully distracting view! Not only can your mind wander in this scenario but your chi is going to be drawn out of the room which can be both tiring and distracting.

The next consideration is where you sit at your desk. All too common in the homes that I have visited is the practical solution of placing the desk or work station up against a wall with many shelves, heavily laden with books up above. From a Feng Shui perspective, this is not the best solution. Firstly, your back is not supported by a mountain (a wall), secondly you are facing a dead end (a wall) and thirdly, there is a great weight of chi bearing down on you from the overladen bookshelves above your work station. I invite you to consider another possible approach. Position your desk so that you are facing out into the room, with your back to a wall and have no sources of cutting chi from the sharp edges of shelves behind your head or shoulders that can make you feel uncomfortable.

Putting these basic principles to work will take you a little bit of time and effort. Although the advice is sound, your space will always be full of contradictions! If you place your desk here, then you are in the draught of chi, if you place your desk on the other side, then you are facing a window! However, take your time and I promise there is a solution somewhere!

The desk itself needs to epitomise your career, your studies and if you are in communication with colleagues and clients from this space, then your capacity to be in touch. First and foremost check the state of your desk. Like your career, this needs to represent stability. Is it rickety, have you jammed pieces of cardboard under one

> *Y*our desk needs to epitomise your career, your studies and if you are in communication with colleagues and clients from this space, your capacity to be in touch.
>
> ✦

leg to level it? Is it a piece of plywood on a couple of old trestle legs? Is it in a poor condition? Have a good, long look at your desk and make sure that it matches up to your dream. Recall when you had an interview with the managing director of a large firm. Did he or she sit in the corner of the room facing a wall operating from a flimsy desk covered in papers and empty cups of tea?

Your chair is your Mountain and vital for your support and concentration. A good chair will keep your chi stable, focused and clear. In many homes that I have visited, the chair at the work station has been a perfect example of 'lack of support'. People have used plastic garden chairs, flimsy typing chairs, an old disused second-hand office chair or, worst of all, a stool or folding chair. Ideally, find a chair that is wonderfully comfortable with a big, broad Mountain of support behind you and ensure that it is in excellent condition. A revolving chair or one that can move on castors, is fine, just so long as it is stable. For an additional aesthetic touch to enhance your chi, look back to the first section of the book regarding astrology and remind yourself which element you are. Look at the previous or supporting element within the cycle and pick a colour that will support your element. You do not need to make the whole chair this colour but perhaps incorporate aspects of it, for example, in a cushion.

Images on the wall of the room where you work can give a subliminal message.

Colours and the Five Elements

- ✦ Soil/Earth – red
- ✦ Metal – yellow
- ✦ Water – white
- ✦ Tree/Wood – blue or black
- ✦ Fire – greens.

Have a look around your space and see what message they are giving you. If you are looking to concentrate, to focus, to internalise and to study, then images of stability are best. If, on the other hand, you are trying to communicate with the outside world, initiate new contacts and initiate contracts, then choose images that are of a more uplifting, outgoing and sociable nature. Many study areas are used for storage. It is fine to keep whatever is current within sight but I strongly advise you to file away papers and material that are relevant to your past, so that they are kept out of your view. Otherwise, on a subliminal level, you are constantly being reminded of the past rather than focusing on the journey ahead of you. If it is vital for your work that you can communicate with the outside world, make sure all the equipment you need for this is in good working order and do not have any time-wasting or irritating features about them. In particular, make sure that the whole communication network of telephone, fax, computer or Internet works simply and effectively. It will all then mirror your career and prospects.

Sources of Negative Chi (External)

- Busy roads
- T-junctions
- Roundabouts
- Railway lines
- Dead trees
- Graveyards
- Stagnant ponds
- Utility poles
- Cutting chi from neighbouring buildings or roofs.

Sources of Negative Chi (Internal)

- Beams
- Draughts of chi
- Accumulated clutter
- Unhealthy plants
- Unhealthy pets
- Sickly occupant
- Cutting chi – from the edges of furniture, appliances, shelves, doorways
- Irregular shaped rooms

Sources of Positive Chi

- Healthy plants
- Healthy fish/aquarium
- Healthy pets
- Healthy occupants
- Lively children
- Fresh air
- Bright lighting
- Clean environment
- Uplifting imagery
- Good circulation of chi

There is more to follow in Chapter 10 regarding other sources of potential stress within the home environment, including electromagnetic pollution, geopathic stress and so on.

Chapter Ten

Feng Shui Fine Tuning

TRADITIONAL **FENG SHUI** is a huge subject to study. A truly skilled practitioner works to harmonise the individual with the influence of Heaven (astrology and divination) and Earth (the landscape, buildings and interior layout). Masters spend a lifetime on such studies. All Feng Shui approaches have one component in common, however, which is that they take care of any negative chi that might be aimed at the property or may be generated internally from sharp angled structures, or draughts of chi as discussed in the previous chapter.

I have chosen in this book to take you through one of the 'layers' of the Compass School known as the Pakua. Even this relatively simple layer of the Compass School can be taken much further in terms of astrology to enable you to use it to plan where best to sleep, work or orientate yourself within the home to achieve more success. The elegance and simplicity of this system lines up with a fundamental understanding of yin and yang, the Five Elements and the significance of the eight trigrams from the *I Ching*.

THE PAKUA

The Pakua is one of the most basic yet versatile and practical tools used in Compass Feng Shui. Derived from the Lo Shu Magic Square, the outline of the Pakua and its sub sections can be superimposed over the floorplan of an entire home, office block – or just one room. Based on the trigrams of the *I Ching*, the Pakua initially provides us with eight sectors which line up with the cardinal and intercardinal points of the compass. Each one of these sectors represents one of the life aspirations which will be outlined in the next section.

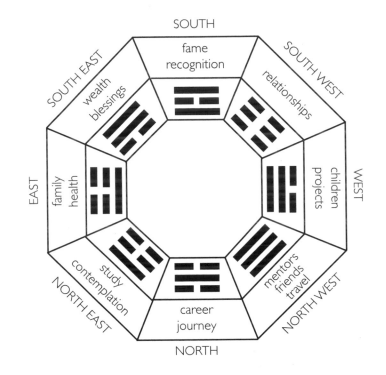

Having assessed your home from a chi perspective in the previous chapter, you can now start to fine tune your space using the ideas and suggestions that follow. It is a very simple and practical application of Compass School Feng Shui which I hope will leave you hungry to delve further into this fascinating and profound approach to Feng Shui. A journey of 1000 miles begins with one step!

STEP 1
Begin by drawing or sketching a fairly accurate floor plan of your home or office, or an individual room. Make sure you clearly indicate where the doors and windows are located, together with staircases and primary pieces of furniture – such as your desk, favourite chair, cooker and bed.

STEP 2

With another colour pen, divide up the floor plan into the nine grids which the Pakua represents. If there is an extension to the property that takes up more than 50 per cent of that side of the building, include it within the Pakua. Although this will leave you with an empty space outside the home, this is still technically to be included within the Pakua (see below). Small extensions of less than 50 per cent of the side of a building or room can be excluded from the Pakua.

STEP 3

Using a simple hand compass, work out which direction is north. Take at least three different readings within the home to ascertain the direction precisely. Once established, mark this on your floor plan with an arrow.

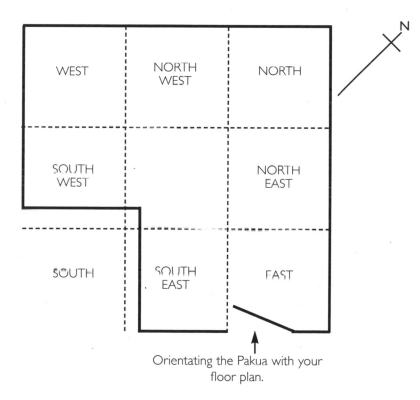

Orientating the Pakua with your
floor plan.

STEP 4

Using a different colour pen, clearly mark on to your floorplan which sector now represents north, south, east, west and the intercardinal directions of north-east, south-east, south-west and north-west. See the diagram on page 165 as an example.

STEP 5

By looking at the Pakua on page 164, observe which part of your home corresponds to a particular life aspiration. For more detail of their symbolism, you need to check the following sections in the text. However, if you are already clear that perhaps your career or studies need working on, notice which sector of your home they occupy or even which sector of a room represents these life aspirations.

STEP 6

In the following sections, look under the various compass points to find which life aspiration you need to work on for your journey. See what you can take from this information and apply it practically to your space. Check whether this sector of your home, in terms of chi, lives up to your current aspirations. For example, does the north-east sector of your home or study provide stillness to support you while you study? Notice whether there is an element of grounding as security while you study. Perhaps the area is very untidy? Perhaps the area is located in a whirlpool of chi where there is little opportunity for stillness or contemplation?

Because of the complementary yet antagonistic nature of yin and yang, it is important to remember that the sector opposite the one you are working on will also need some attention. What has a front, has a back and also the bigger the front, the bigger the back. For example, if you are working on the north-east sector, check the south-west sector too, which is associated with relationships. While the north-east is about stillness, contemplation and technically being 'out of relationship' with the outside world, too much emphasis will invariably drain your relationship with others. Do not put all your eggs in one basket by concentrating on one sector and paying little or no attention to its complementary yet antagonistic opposite sector.

NORTHERN SECTOR

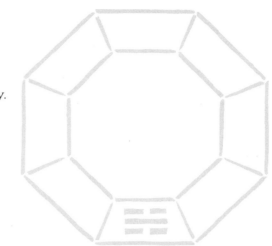

LIFE ASPIRATION: Career/journey.

TRIGRAM: K'an.

ELEMENT: Water.

COLOUR: Blue, black.

SYMBOLISM

As in the natural world, water needs to flow unhindered for it to be fresh, vital and inspiring. Bringing out this symbolism in this sector involves keeping the area uncluttered and creating a sense of meandering movement. It is best to encourage a flow of water energy rather than a cascade, dam up the energy or allow it to stagnate.

QUESTIONS TO ASK YOURSELF

Regarding your career, prospects and inner journey in life, ask yourself the following questions. Do you feel that you are in tune with, or lined up with your dream? Do you feel that you are on target regarding your long-term plans? Do you feel energised in your work? Are new prospects coming your way? Does your career feel stable at present? Are you losing contracts and opportunities? Do you feel that you are being overlooked by your colleagues, clients or boss?

SUPPORT FOR THIS SECTOR

Colours that reflect this water element are of a darker nature – dark blues and even black. Images of seascapes, flowing water, or fish subliminally support this sector A water feature or fish tank that fits proportionately within this space could be appropriate. The basic design and layout of this sector needs to have a natural 'flowing' quality to it. No sharp edges and a peaceful, uncluttered environment is best.

IF SECTOR MISSING

In Chinese medicine, water represents the health, vitality and chi of our kidneys, bladder and reproductive system. It is regarded as the root of our vitality. With this sector missing, it is quite possible that you have less vitality, feel tired, run down, vulnerable and withdrawn.

SECTOR ENLARGED

The profound nature of water in relation to our chi is its capacity to reflect. Naturally, with a larger northern sector, your intuitive and psychic capacities will be more charged. In terms of career, you could be more successful in a field of work that relies on deep reflection, patient judgement and good intuition.

FRONT DOOR FACING NORTH

In this situation your door is facing the winter, the cold and stillness. Occupants of this home are more likely to feel the cold, to become more withdrawn or isolated and potentially anxious over threats from the outside world. The chill winds of chi that the north can generate encourage you and other occupants to hibernate rather than to socialise.

NORTH-EASTERN SECTOR

LIFE ASPIRATION: Knowledge/contemplation.

TRIGRAM: K'en.

ELEMENT: Earth.

COLOUR: Beige.

SYMBOLISM

The trigram K'en symbolises the Mountain – stillness, contemplation and hidden inner strength. It can also represent our inner knowledge and our capacity to study. In an ideal world, this sector of your home or sector of a room would ideally be used as a study or a meditation room. You need to create an atmosphere of stillness, grounding and stability.

QUESTIONS TO ASK YOURSELF

Do you need more time and space for your own self-development? Do you find too many demands placed on your time at work and insufficient time left for yourself? Are you very distracted with your career, family life or social life and need time and space for yourself? If you are studying for exams, are you constantly distracted? Do you need stability, inspiration or motivation at present regarding your own studies?

SUPPORT FOR THIS SECTOR

In an ideal world, you would place your desk either in the north-east sector of your home or the north-east sector of a room. Support the imagery of a Mountain and stillness by paintings and images that support this. No photographs of Formula 1 racing cars spinning off the track! The best colours are beige, darker blues and darker shades of green.

Knowledge and self-development is about our inner hunger and thirst. You can represent this by having an empty receptacle close by to symbolise receptivity. For example, you can choose an earthenware vessel, such as a vase, a trinket box, or a decorative bowl. If you are looking for inspiration, incorporate lighting that is drawn from the Fire element, such as candles or uplighters. Remember that in the Five Element theory, Fire supports Soil/Earth.

IF SECTOR IS MISSING

Without this sector, it will undoubtedly be difficult for you to study, to maintain stillness or even to concentrate on meditation or other spiritual practices. You may be drawn to studying in a library, reading in your favourite coffee shop or finding a peaceful space somewhere else in the community.

IF SECTOR IS ENLARGED

In this situation the occupants of the home are likely to become isolated and insular in their own world. There will be tendency for everybody to do their own thing. With over emphasis on the presence of Mountain within the home, communication problems are likely to arise. It will be difficult for everyone to communicate their feelings and, at the same time, much harder for them to hear the needs of others.

IF FRONT DOOR IS FACING THE NORTH-EAST

Frequently, the most foreboding and threatening cold winds come from the northeast. Opening your front door every morning to the icy blasts of a Siberian gale is hardly the most auspicious start! The strong, deep and penetrating nature of chi from the north-east can lead to health problems such as colds, lingering infections, bronchial disorders and flu-type symptoms. It is also quite likely that women will find it far more difficult to conceive in a home where the front door faces the north-east.

EASTERN SECTOR

LIFE ASPIRATION: Family and health.

TRIGRAM: Chen.

COLOUR: Green, dark green.

SYMBOLISM

The trigram Chen is frequently transliterated as 'Thunder' or the 'Arousing'. As east represents dawn and the initiation of new activity, it symbolises our health, our vitality and our family roots. It is an active sector of the home which represents the charge of chi we receive from behind us from our lineage as well as our vitality and stamina that we bring into the world reflected through our health.

Family, in this sense, can go beyond immediate family and represent the 'tribe' that we belong to. In modern times, we may all belong to several different tribes – sports club, golf club, workplace, charity, and so on.

Health in this context is more associated with spontaneity, flexibility and vitality.

QUESTIONS TO ASK YOURSELF

How would you rate your current relationship with your parents? Are you in communication with them? Are they supportive and understanding of your journey in life? If one or both of your parents have passed on, ask yourself whether you had a good relationship with them at the time of their passing. Are you grateful and inspired by their contribution to your life? How do you get on with your bosses? Are you being recognised, encouraged and supported by them at present? How is your health? Do you have good vitality? Are you hungry and curious to discover more on your journey?

SUPPORT FOR THIS SECTOR

Drawing on the imagery of dawn or spring or the initiation of any project, then think no further than the imagery of Wood/Tree. Its chi is best expressed by fresh, healthy plants. Energise the sector with plants, good lighting and fresh air. Remember, that within the Five Element cycle, Wood/Tree is supported by Water and it may be appropriate to have a small water feature in this sector.

Include colours in this sector of dark green, light blue or turquoise. Install imagery that represents the dawn, freshness and vibrant health.

Photographs, paintings or images of your 'tribe' help to support this sector. These could be photographs of your family, your work colleagues or members of your team at the sports club. However, try to restrict the number and size of photographs and paintings of your ancestors who have passed on. Our journey is designed to be a forward looking adventure rather than a retrospective one.

IF SECTOR IS MISSING

This brings with it the possibility of poor health, low vitality and little appetite for creativity. There could also be a tendency towards being out of touch with your 'tribe' – your parents, their relatives, your work colleagues and friends.

IF SECTOR IS ENLARGED

This brings a very positive charge to all the members of the household. Possibilities include heightened vitality, greater enthusiasm and positive relationships with family, friends and colleagues.

FRONT DOOR FACING EAST

Here the chi of the dawn is brought right into your home. This is particularly auspicious if you are trying to initiate a new career, a new project or attempting to diversify, extend or build on existing project. This spring-like chi will be particularly beneficial to the children of the household as they occupy and live through the dawn of their life and journey.

THE SOUTH-EASTERN SECTOR

LIFE ASPIRATION: Prosperity and luck.

TRIGRAM: Sun.

ELEMENT: Small Tree/Wood

COLOUR: Green, light green.

SYMBOLISM

The south-eastern sector of your home brings with it the warmest sunshine and invigorating chi. From a seasonal perspective, it represents the late spring when plant life is in its most abundant phase, producing blossom. This is a powerful sector of your home that brings with it not just the potential for luck, prosperity and wealth but also good health. Enhancing this sector can really help make miracles happen. As we have all learnt on our journey, luck is often about being in the right place at the right time and being open to new possibilities. Keep this sector bright and fresh giving you a window for new opportunities to occur.

QUESTIONS TO ASK YOURSELF

How is your luck at present? Are plenty of opportunities coming your way? Do you feel you are being overlooked and left out at present? Do others around you seem to be more lucky than you? How is your financial situation? Do you have a healthy cash flow? Do you have adequate savings for the future? Are you open to a life of surprises and opportunities that could lead to prosperity and success?

SUPPORT FOR THIS SECTOR

For most of us, this sector of the home (in the northern hemisphere) receives some of the best sunshine of the day. Plants will thrive in this sector and also represent the Tree/Wood element. In particular, look at purchasing a healthy money plant, also known as the jade plant or *Crasula argenta*. These hardy succulents need little water and with time grow steadily and potentially can blossom up to twice a year.

The element Water supports this sector so you may choose to consider a water feature – especially one with flowing water, such as an indoor fountain. The colours should be light greens and mixtures of greens and blues, including mauve, light purple and light burgundy.

Images that are uplifting, energising and inspiring help to promote this sector. This is definitely not the area to keep your excess baggage, unwanted newspapers or waste basket!

IF SECTOR IS MISSING

Without this sector you may find yourself down on your luck and struggling financially. You may well be on the sidelines while others seem to have all the success and opportunities. There may also be unnecessary drains on your financial resources — high rent, high maintenance costs, high demands on your pocket or even legal costs that drain your cash.

IF SECTOR IS ENLARGED

Here the sky is the limit with a huge potential for success, luck, prosperity and good health. Opportunities could literally swamp you. However, take care not to take on too much in too many directions as this could drain your energy, vitality and reserves in the long term.

FRONT DOOR FACING SOUTH-EAST

Chi from the south-east entering your home will promote a very active, happy, energetic environment. This is especially good for maintaining contacts and good communication with the outside world which can lead to new projects and endeavours. Getting projects started and allowing new opportunities to enter your life will not be a problem. However, you need to make sure you are well organised to see them through to their fruition.

SOUTHERN SECTOR

LIFE ASPIRATION: Recognition and fame.

TRIGRAM: Li.

ELEMENT: Fire.

COLOUR: Red.

SYMBOLISM

This sector represents recognition and acknowledgement for what you have achieved. The Element Fire brings with it the chi of wisdom, clarity, brilliance, perception and intuition. This sector not only helps to inspire us internally but gets us noticed externally at the same time. Fire can often express the full potential of our dream and the success of our journey.

QUESTIONS TO ASK YOURSELF

Do you have a special skill that you wish to be recognised? Have you devised a product that needs good marketing? Are you getting the recognition you deserve? What do you wish to be known for? Are others, possibly less talented than yourself, getting all the recognition? Do you feel that you are being overlooked? Do you feel that your efforts are not being recognised as a parent? Do you feel left out of your community? Are you being overlooked in your relationships?

SUPPORT FOR THIS SECTOR

Fire truly represents light in all its manifestations. It is essential that this sector of your room or home is well lit – whether by conventional lighting or using candles. You only have to notice the uplifting and energising effect that the chi of a natural fire has when you enter a room to appreciate this.

In terms of colour, bring in various shades of red including purples, pinks, maroons and burgundies. Keep the colours bright and vibrant and get rid of any lacklustre decorations that diminish the chi of Fire.

Place within this sector something that represents what you wish to be known for. This might be a diploma from college, a trophy you won, a work of art that you created or a letter of acknowledgement. Focus these images carefully as, after all, Fire represents clarity. If you are well known for being a poor time keeper, consider placing a clock in this sector with hour, minute and second hands to keep you in order! Wood/Tree is the supporter of Fire, therefore plants are beneficial in this sector. Given that they are facing the South, they will also benefit from the maximum amount of sunlight that this sector receives.

IF SECTOR IS MISSING

This can result in a lack of recognition or acknowledgement. In turn this will leave you lacking self-esteem and confidence. Your talent and creativity can easily be overlooked.

IF SECTOR IS ENLARGED

No worries here, you will be famous! You have enormous potential to be recognised not only for your creativity but also for your wisdom, clarity and intuition.

IF FRONT DOOR IS FACING SOUTH

A full blast of Fire entering your home is going to activate the house and its occupants. You are likely to feel more sociable, lively, outgoing and fun. There is a word of caution however. Fire naturally illuminates whatever is present and tends to exaggerate what is 'lit up' within its presence. Stagnation and dust will only magnify. If you already feel unhappy or lacking in confidence, Fire can exaggerate these feelings. Remember that Fire charges any atmosphere and, on a negative level, this can spark off stormy arguments as well as passionate romances!

SOUTH-WESTERN SECTOR

LIFE ASPIRATION: Marriage and relationships.

TRIGRAM: K'un.

ELEMENT: Big Earth.

COLOUR: Yellow, brown.

SYMBOLISM

The trigram K'un represents the full force of yin energy which creates the imagery of receptivity. This is the most yin, or the most open, of all the trigrams. It is also the most feminine of all the trigrams, governed by the element Earth which brings with it an essence of warmth, love, caring and relationship with others.

Relationship in this context can be portrayed as marriage, relationships with family and friends, colleagues and neighbours. This sector of the home not only reflects our current relationships but also our potential to form new relationships or to make old relationships more enduring.

QUESTIONS TO ASK YOURSELF

Are you in a good relationship with your boss and your colleagues at work? Are you in communication with old friends? What is your relationship with your clients at present? Is there harmony and balance between you and your neighbours? How would you rate your relationship/marriage at present? Is there stability in the relationship? Is there a future in the relationship?

SUPPORT FOR THIS SECTOR

Naturally, keep this sector of your home, or room – and especially your bedroom – clear of unwanted debris and dust. To energise this sector. which is supported by the element Earth/Soil, you could use natural crystals. The element Fire is the creator of Soil/Earth and it would be appropriate to place candles or images of Fire in this sector. Try to create an environment that is inviting, warm and safe in this sector. In many homes that I have visited, the occupants have intuitively chosen this sector as their lounge, seating area or dining area.

Colours that support this sector include yellow and mild shades of red such as pink or mauve. A photograph of you and your partner is ideal to place in this sector or, if you are looking to form a new relationship, figurines and paintings of couples, or pairs of birds, can provide the subliminal stimulation for this sector.

IF SECTOR IS MISSING

Given that this part of your home or room is strongly influenced by yin, the feminine principle, women in particular are going to feel more uncomfortable than men in this home. Since the Earth's yin energy is the fundamental charging chi for women, with this sector missing, it is likely to leave them feeling tired and isolated and they may even develop health problems.

IF SECTOR ENLARGED

With a large south-western aspect of the home, women are going to feel happy, comfortable and energised. Overall, the home will have a feeling of warmth, relaxation and receptivity to others. It could well become a gathering place for your family, friends and neighbours.

FRONT DOOR FACING SOUTH-WEST

The chi that comes from the south-west has the mellow energy of the late afternoon. It is the time of day when chi begins to settle and consolidate. It can easily create an atmosphere of warmth and contentment. Looking at it as the 'late afternoon' of our own lifespan, it could also represent retirement. This could be an ideal home for a couple beginning a long and mellow retirement.

WESTERN SECTOR

LIFE ASPIRATION: Children/projects.

TRIGRAM: Tui.

ELEMENT: Small Metal.

COLOUR: White, silver and grey.

SYMBOLISM

Sitting in the west, the chi that stimulates this sector is both profoundly reflective and potentially creative. The late afternoon and early evening are generally times when our chi consolidates, we reflect on our day's activities and we are inspired to bring new levels of energy to our creativity. For those with families, children represent true creativity in any relationship. They are a manifestation of our chi, our love and our blood. In a similar vein, our future projects, schemes, dreams and creations can fall into the same category. New projects that we undertake as they develop and grow are indeed our 'children'. The trigram Tui (Lake/Joy) has always been associated with warmth, communication and fun.

QUESTIONS TO ASK YOURSELF

How is your relationship with your children? If they are young, are they succeeding well at school or college? How is their health, creativity? Do you feel creative at present? Are your plans developing fruitfully? Do you need inspiration or motivation with your creativity? Are you having a fun, active social life?

SUPPORT FOR THIS SECTOR

Whether you are looking at a sector of your home or simply the western sector of your main lounge, try to create an ambience that is relaxing and inspiring to you. You can help achieve this by using comfortable, sumptuous seating, soft lighting, keeping your stereo system here, and including relaxing and inspiring paintings and images. This is a very sensorial sector of your home. Keep your most favourite works of art, sculpture or bronzes in this sector. Play the kind of music that inspires you. Keep at hand the kinds of books that give you new ideas.

This is the perfect area to display photographs of your children and grandchildren, together with any examples of their own creativity and success. To support the Metal element, consider using colours that are close to white, including silver, grey, gold and cream.

IF SECTOR IS MISSING

With Metal governing this sector and being representative of money, the occupants may have problems with cash flow. Even with a lucrative income, the outgoings could easily match or exceed earnings. There is the potential for difficulties with children, such as an inability to conceive, and children's health problems or academic difficulties. From a social perspective, the occupants could feel isolated, stuck and possibly depressed.

IF SECTOR IS ENLARGED

In this situation the house is fully charged on a more social level. A wonderful home to host memorable parties and social gatherings! Children will also be highly charged in this space, making many friends, and the local children will be particularly attracted to this home. Parents need to be warned that there will be lots of phone calls, children dropping by, parties and sleepovers!

FRONT DOOR FACING WEST

A very lively, creative, fun atmosphere is supported by the chi from the west. If you are single, there will be romance and many opportunities for friendships and relationships. From a financial perspective, you can expect a generous income, however it will be matched with equally demanding outgoings – especially on non-essential items such as holidays and clothes.

NORTH-WESTERN SECTOR

LIFE ASPIRATION: Helpful friends and mentors.

TRIGRAM: Ch'ien.

ELEMENT: Big Metal.

COLOUR: Gold, white, metallic shades.

SYMBOLISM

The trigram Ch'ien represents the full force of yang – Heaven. It is a powerful sector within the home and represents your connection with the outside world including your mentors, supportive colleagues and friends, networking, travel and international business prospects. The authority of Heaven implies a sense of respect and love of those who have supported you on your journey. This sector suggests stability, strength and clarity.

QUESTIONS TO ASK YOURSELF

From a business perspective, how is your communication with clients and producers? Are you getting enquiries and orders from abroad? Do you feel left out of the loop? Are you in good communication with your friends or teachers? Are your neighbours helpful? Are you giving time to your community? Do you participate in any charitable work? How efficient is your current communication system – telephone, fax and e-mail?

SUPPORT FOR THIS SECTOR

This is the ideal part of your home or office to place your communications centre, whether merely a telephone or a more sophisticated system. When you work from home it can be especially hard to maintain communication with the outside world, so make every effort to stimulate this sector favourably. During office hours, try keeping a light on in this sector. If you are attempting to initiate sales abroad, consider placing a globe here. Decor that supports Metal includes all shades of white, cream, silver, grey and gold. Solid yang metallic objects such as bronzes bring stability to this sector. Crystals, from the Soil/Earth element will also help to support the Metal element. Keep the sector clear of all dust, dirt, debris and wastepaper baskets. Avoid using candles as Fire melts Metal within the Five Elements system.

IF SECTOR IS MISSING

The masculine nature of Ch'ien would have a more adverse effect on the male occupants of the home. It is quite likely that they will have difficulties in communicating with the outside world, and find a lack of support from friends, mentors and colleagues. Without a strong charge of yang, they could be left low in energy, vitality and stamina. They are more likely to have lingering health problems as the result of colds and flu.

IF SECTOR IS ENLARGED

The chi of the north-west and its full force of yang can potentially be overbearing. If well channelled, this chi could improve your communication and your potential for clients abroad. On the other hand, too much yang stimulating the space could leave you feeling isolated and out of touch with your friends.

IF FRONT DOOR IS FACING NORTH-WEST

This has a very powerful and beneficial effect on the male occupants of the home. The full masculine force of Heaven coming into the home brings a sense of respect and dominion to the Father of the household. His position in the community will be well respected and his advice from colleagues and friends will be frequently sought.

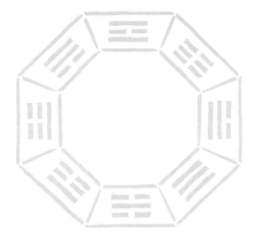

CENTRE

THE CENTRAL SECTOR of your home or room relates to the harmony and balance of the whole building. All the other eight sectors interplay and interrelate through this central sector. East and west, south-west and north-east, and so on, all balance each other. You can achieve this balance by keeping this central sector free of debris or heavy furniture. Chi energy needs to flow unhindered through your space and by blocking this portion of the room, you are also not allowing the different sectors to interact. An exception to this would be if a view from a window proves a major distraction when you enter a particular room. There could be cutting chi entering through the window, an unsightly vista, or a large blank wall. By placing a focus in the centre of the room such as a beautiful rug, or a low coffee table with a central ornament, your eye is distracted from the view while it focuses on this feature.

Any furniture placed in the centre of the room needs to be fairly unobtrusive and certainly should not have any sharp edges that would cause cutting chi. Check the light fixture in the centre of the room or your home. Many modern lampshades and fittings come to a sharp point at the base. This creates a downward arrowhead pointing at the floor, which is a disturbing source of cutting chi. Having cutting chi right in the centre of your room does not set the tone! Colours that support this central sector, which is associated with the element Earth/Soil, would be the various shades of yellow including orange, gold and light brown.

CONCLUSION

LESS IS MORE – try not to make too many changes initially. A few well intentioned remedies in place and left for a period of 10 – 30 days are far better than 20 remedies that you constantly fiddle and tweak with.

Try a selection of the remedies that are mentioned in Chapter 9.

Before finely tuning your space as outlined in this chapter, do remember to set the tone by dealing with any cutting chi from the previous chapter.

The chi is strongest in the home around noon – between the hours of 11 am and 1 pm – a very good time to put in place any Feng Shui remedies.

Chapter Eleven

Avoiding Hidden Hazards on Your Journey

THE APPLICATION OF TRADITIONAL Feng Shui practice and principles into your life can undoubtedly be of major benefit. Although intrinsically the natural world has changed little over the past millennium, there are many new potential hazards within our homes and our immediate environment that were not present when much of the wisdom of Feng Shui was put down on paper centuries ago. To make our homes more comfortable and healthy today, we can now draw on traditional practices from all over the world and benefit from new research regarding environmental hazards and potentially dangerous modern building materials. Although this may seem like very new problems, these points have been appreciated for centuries, not only in China but in many other traditional cultures in the world.

Living as we do in a yang phase of humanity's development where science is the dominant leader, most theories have to be subjected to the rigorous testing of Cartesian and Newtonian laws. However, Feng Shui and its associated disciplines come from a more yin appreciation of ourselves, our environment and our destiny. It is hard, though not impossible, therefore to measure much of this valuable wisdom from today's analytical yang perspective. Much of the following is common sense, and many people are already intuitively practising it. All these systems are intended to enhance the vibrational level of the home and to promote a supportive atmosphere that can pervade our health, fortune and journey.

EXCESS BAGGAGE

EVERY POSSESSION IN the home has its own vibrational quality. Everything we buy, every gift we receive and any family heirloom we inherit all contain their own particular frequencies. In an ideal world, we surround ourselves with artefacts, furniture and possessions that have either a functional use or are aesthetically pleasing to the soul. Surrounding ourselves with objects that we are not happy with, that are broken, out of date, or that we seldom use are simply taking up space. Excess baggage in the home has the potential to slow down our chi, limit our perspective of a new bright future and, to a certain degree, connect us more with our past than with our future.

I highly recommend Karen Kingston's book *Clear Your Clutter with Feng Shui* which gives an excellent overview of the benefits of keeping your home clear of unwanted possessions. Before making any well-intentioned Feng Shui changes in your home, clear the decks of all excess baggage to maximise the potential for new changes to occur in your home and your life. There are three stages to undertaking this important task:

1. Dealing with the physical excess baggage in your home.

2. Dealing with the vibrational or outstanding emotional issues in your life.

3. Drawing from the suggestions in Section 3 where you can begin to work on your health and well-being.

STEP ONE
You need to be ruthless. Make a note of your possessions, going through the house room by room and be clear about what you use on a regular basis. Excess baggage is material that is either redundant, broken or has been waiting several months or years to be repaired! Old clothes, unwanted gifts, out of date magazines, old college notes, broken gadgets all fall into this category. Clothing, utensils and tools that you use on a seasonal basis are not regarded as excess baggage and can be stored away conveniently and brought out when appropriate. Try to avoid an old mistake of filling your attic or basement with boxes of junk that you promise yourself you will go through one day. Be ruthless!

If you are young or single, living in rented accommodation, think where you may have stored your excess baggage? Did you leave it in your parents' attic? Have you left it in the basement of your brother's home? If so, you need to work on this as well as, in the long term, it is not going to do them any good. Have friends, a neighbour or relative taken a job abroad and left trunks and suitcases of their baggage in your loft? If you are unclear how long you are expected to store their 'excess', contact them and clarify this point. If it looks like it is going to be a vague ongoing process, you need to be clear and get it sorted.

STEP TWO

We can easily slow down our progress in life by being too caught up with the past. On an emotional or vibrational level, reflect on what outstanding business there may be in your life. Pay particular attention to any outstanding or incomplete conversations you have had with a friend, relative, business colleague or an ex-love. Unresolved issues in our lives are very similar to untidy desks with mountains of paper work! Clearing the air, clearing the desk opens up possibilities. Take a moment to draw up a list of those you need to phone, write to, or have coffee with to resolve any misunderstanding or outstanding issues.

STEP THREE

The Metal element in Oriental healing relates to the lungs and large intestines. Both of these organs are responsible for absorbing aspects of the external world within us, as well as being responsible for the elimination of excess. The health and the efficiency of these two vital organs is naturally reflected in how well we deal with excess baggage in the world around us. Chronic breathing difficulties or digestive problems inevitably lead to a deeper physical stagnation within us and a darker, gloomier outlook on life. In other words, stagnation sets in.

If you feel this is an issue with you, look back at the material in Part 3 and review the advice that deals with strengthening the Metal element in your life. In addition to those suggestions, make cleaning a daily ritual rather than a daily chore. Done briskly, on a reasonably empty stomach, energetically and with some uplifting music in the background, you can get the job done while at the same time recharging your chi. For my first year as a student of the Oriental healing arts in the 1970s, I had a part-time job as a cleaner. Looking back, it was the most care-free, enjoyable, invigorating and satisfying job I think I have ever held. Although a humble position, in many ways I was responsible for setting the tone of the building. It is not uncommon today to find monks who dedicate their lives to spiritual practices in monasteries, interspersing their days of study with bursts of energetic cleaning.

Naturally, prevention is considered the best cure among all the great healing systems. Keep your home brightly charged and clear of unwanted baggage and you open the doors to new possibilities. Surround yourself with junk, debris, dust and old chi and you simply attract more of the same. Do you recall as a child that you would never dream of walking across your parent's sparkling clean kitchen floor? However, if it was dirty and covered in smudge marks, you wouldn't think twice about it because your muddy footprints would not be noticed so much! Walking through a leafy litter-free suburb, you would not expect to find anyone throwing rubbish on to the pavement. However, if there is a vacant plot where somebody has already dumped some rubbish, before long you will find everyone else is doing the same. Simply speaking, this is called 'big yin attracts little yin!'

SPACE CLEARING

SPACE CLEARING IS A ritual found in almost every traditional or native culture in the world. It is a powerful skill that enables the practitioner to change the atmosphere of the home from one of stagnant chi to one of vibrant health, promoting and spiritually enhancing chi. In traditional cultures, space clearing, or having your home blessed, has always been considered a vital measure when moving into a new home. In the West, it is more likely to be linked to having a good spring clean, a housewarming party or to have your local priest bless the home.

Typically, when the body's own chi becomes acutely stagnant, symptoms can include irritability, tiredness, lack of enthusiasm or stamina, and depression. Given that we are active beings and that the condition is acute, it is relatively simple to change stagnant chi. A good night's sleep, a bracing walk, a cool shower or a hot drink can all change your chi relatively quickly. However, the chi of a building can take much longer to change as it absorbs stagnant chi on a much deeper level. Building materials such as bricks, concrete, steel, stone and wood are much more yang than people, taking longer to absorb energy and longer to discharge. A simple way of being aware of this chi is to visit any major public building – a library, hospital, church or town hall. Over the years, the chi energy related to the activity of the occupants has slowly been absorbed into the building. The atmosphere can be totally different from that of a fairly modern primary school where the materials used are lighter and softer – more yin – and where the occupants, children, are vital, fresh, curious, energetic and stimulating to the environment.

The purpose of space clearing is to break up any stagnant chi within the home, refresh it, stabilise it and 'announce' your presence. Here are some practical examples of space clearing that could be considered a vital part of uplifting the chi of your home, clearing the way to a bright fresh future on your journey.

PRACTICAL SPACE CLEARING

1. CLEARING THE PREDECESSOR CHI.

When you move into a new home or office, it is important to consider who occupied the space before you. Their health, happiness, and chi has all rubbed off in the space. Even if the new home is stripped bare of all the furnishings, their chi will still remain. This predecessor chi will be strongest where they slept, where they sat, and along the 'pathways' that they created as they walked around the rooms. On the other hand, there will be parts of the room or home that they did not use. This could be a spare bedroom or a corner of a room where a piece of furniture stood that hid a corner, thereby not allowing chi to circulate easily.

I have often been curious whether political leaders have considered using space clearing. Imagine moving into the White House or 10 Downing Street not only as a new leader but with a new party that had previously been in opposition. In some cases, immediately after the elections, the new party takes office in exactly the same space as their predecessor. Apart from changing the furniture, having a good party and probably a few laughs at their predecessor's fate, what do these leaders do to bring their new intention to the space?

2. AFTER PHYSICAL OR PSYCHOLOGICAL ILLNESS.

If you or someone in your home has been ill for a considerable period, the vibration of the home will be affected. When someone is seriously ill at home, the daily routine is affected, the occupants' social life is often inhibited and there is an atmosphere of stillness, quietness and nervous apprehension. For the person who has been ill, there may have been suffering, pain and anxiety. For the occupants who share the space, their energy naturally becomes more subdued.

In the same way that a good traditional nurse would fling open the curtains in the morning, make you get out of bed while they refresh the sheets and puff up the pillows, open the windows, and bring in fresh flowers, we need to change the chi. Space clearing after physical or psychological illness will undoubtedly improve the chi of the home and set the tone for a fresh, bright future.

3. AFTER BIG LIFE CHANGES

Stress from today's hectic lifestyle can affect all of us. The most powerful causes of 'dis-stress' include divorce, bereavement, end of a relationship, loss of job or change of career. Once we have come to terms with our grief, frustration or anger, it is time to move on. Rather than living in an atmosphere of chi that is charged by the past, it is important, when appropriate, to go forward. There is no progress to be had in hanging on to the past and, from a Feng Shui point of view, what we are actually hanging on to is chi. There is no physical presence of the person we have lost, no physical manifestation of the job we may have lost or have changed. These memories only lie within ourselves and they can manifest in our chi which, in turn, can be absorbed by our environment.

4. AFTER CONFLICT IN THE HOME

Burglary or, worse, assault in your home creates an atmosphere of chi that needs to be cleared. The space has been violated and many people report feeling uncomfortable when entering their home after such an event. On a lesser level, if you have had violent arguments within the home recently, these have undoubtedly left their mark on the atmosphere. Constant bickering and fighting for months or years on end allows this negative chi to seep into the space and almost create an atmosphere that supports further disharmony.

5. MAKING A FRESH START IN LIFE

Having a clear idea of where you want to go and what you want to do is fine, but unless this is supported by your surroundings, you may feel that your path is easily blocked. Setting the tone for a new enterprise or relationship can be vital to its success. It is very easy to separate work from home in our minds. Imagine you have been promoted at work; you are excited and feel challenged about it. Naturally, you will know what to do from the work point of view but what can your home environment provide to support you in this process? Your work, creativity and potential outside of the home is naturally supported by where you live. As with any new relationship, clear away the past cobwebs to allow fresh new possibilities into your life.

WHAT IS INVOLVED

THERE ARE AS MANY different methods of space clearing as there are cultures in the world. The rituals that have been used include the use of herbs, chants, potions, symbolism, spiritual ceremonies, blessings, sacrifices, gifts, fruits, plants, holy water and sometimes the timing of the event to coincide with the planets or moon cycles. Space clearing can be drawn from the Native American medicine wheel, Celtic ceremonies, early Christian rituals and Balinese methods. For further insights into how to utilise space clearing in your lives, I highly recommend Karen Kingston's book *Creating Sacred Space* with Feng Shui or Denise Linn's book *Sacred Space*.

There are usually three steps involved in space clearing.

STEP 1

Firstly, it is vital to give the home a really good spring clean and, at the same time, remove all clutter. Following on from this is the use of ritual to further purify the space. This can involve any of the following four elements: Water – holy water, energised water or purified water; Fire – candles or an open fire; Earth – plants, flowers, crystals or salt; Air – essential oils, incense, feathers, Native American smudge sticks, bells, drums, music or chanting.

Offerings are usually made by placing these elements in different parts of the home. A skilled practitioner will usually start at the front door, moving from room to room, using one of the Air elements, such as incense, drumming or chanting to move the chi.

STEP 2

The second step, once the space has been cleared, is to refine and uplift the atmosphere of the home. This is usually done with a good quality bell, or with music, clapping, prayer or chanting.

STEP 3

The third and equally vital step, is to set the 'intention' of the space. Once the space has been cleared, it has been raised to a higher vibrational level and, rather like a void, is ready to be filled. This moment provides an opportunity to set the tone of the new space. Chi energy will always follow intention. Some kind of ceremony is important now to establish this. This is often carried out by standing at the centre of each room and allowing your energy to expand and fill the space while, at the same time, declaring your intention.

Space clearing is not recommended when your chi is low or you feel run down or ill. It is never wise to space clear someone else's home, as this is much better left to a professional. Details of how to contact a professional space clearer are available in the resource section at the back of this book.

ELECTROMAGNETIC POLLUTION

OUR FENG SHUI forbears had no idea of the kinds of hazards future generations would create for themselves in today's buildings. Electromagnetic fields (EMFs) do occur at mild levels in the natural world. However, current research suggests that we are now being bombarded with the equivalent of 200 million times the amount of electromagnetic pollution that our forbears had to face. Given that our cellular structure is charged by chi, chemicals and electrical charges, these high levels of electromagnetic pollution are bound to affect us. Even those blessed with strong constitutions and healthy immune systems can have lapses of memory, increased tiredness and frequent headaches. However, those with weaker immune systems are likely to be far more susceptible to infections and the development of chronic diseases.

Sources of EMF can range from electricity pylons, which can transmit their effect over a distance of up to ¼ mile down to the humble bedside electric clock which can project its EMF up to 6 feet (1.8 metres) away. Other sources of EMF that have crept into our homes in the past few generations include electric cookers, washing machines, hair dryers, microwave ovens, stereo systems, digital clocks, televisions, computers, electric razors, fluorescent lighting and mobile telephones. Even the precious stones in our jewellery can pick up EMFs and transfer them to us via the meridians and acupuncture points along the fingers, and around the neck, wrists and ears.

One of the priorities of Feng Shui is to deal with any source of negative chi – Sha Chi – so it is important to check your home and office for major sources of electromagnetic pollution. As with Sha Chi, your main aim should be to avoid it. Primarily, this means checking the areas where you spend most of your life – your desk, bed and favourite armchair. As a general rule, it is wise to turn off all electrical appliances when they are not in use and to remove the plug from the socket. Definitely avoid sleeping close to a night storage heater and avoid having a 'spaghetti junction' of live electric cables within 6 feet (1.8 metres) of your bed. Harmful EMFs from television sets can radiate up to 10 feet (3 metres). I certainly do not recommend keeping a television in the bedroom! If you have young or even teenage children, consider checking for sources of EMFs around the bed. The amount of electrical gadgetry that is part of a youngster's life nowadays is enormous compared to previous genera-tions. Excessive amounts of EMFs are not only going to affect their health but also their concentration and moods.

Roger Coghill, a leading authority on electromagnetic stress and author of Elec-tromagnetic Pollution has researched the subject in depth and has made available a relatively small and inexpensive diagnostic tool called a FieldMouse (details in the Resource Section). The FieldMouse can help you check for safe levels of EMFs within the home – and it certainly gives a new perspective on those seemingly quiet, inoffensive domestic appliances we share our homes with!

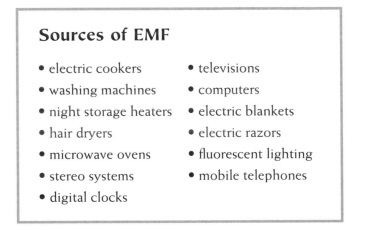

Sources of EMF

- electric cookers
- washing machines
- night storage heaters
- hair dryers
- microwave ovens
- stereo systems
- digital clocks
- televisions
- computers
- electric blankets
- electric razors
- fluorescent lighting
- mobile telephones

One of the best ways to reduce EMFs within the home would be to have an elec-trician fit a gadget that automatically cuts off the electric current at the mains when you are not using any appliances. This would create a far better environment in the bedroom and minimises your use of electricity at the same time. Contact Coghill Research (see Resource Section) – Electromagnetic Stress Detectors and Eliminators for advice and information on the availability of their product. There are two devices that I can recommend for eliminating or neutralising electromagnetic pollution within the home. They both plug into an electric socket and also help with geopathic stress (see below).

1. RadiTech – available from the Dulwich Health Society (see Resource List).

2. Helios 1 – available from Jan Cisek (see Resource List).

In the past 20 years there has been increased research into the effects of building materials on our health. This whole approach is gaining more credibility and is the latest development in 'building ecology'. It involves greater understanding and careful use of building materials, on the basis that the home is a living and breathing organism. Research shows that building materials and insulation materials and paints not only contain toxic materials but that some materials also give off low grade radioactivity which they discharge over a long period of time. Intuition and common sense must prevail as our experience of living with these new potential hazards only goes back one or two generations. For more insights and a fuller understanding of this subject, refer to the Reference Section on building ecology.

GEOPATHIC STRESS

MUCH CREDIBLE SCIENTIFIC research has been done on geopathic stress in the past 17 years and it is becoming increasingly clear that this subject needs to be taken seriously by the home owner. Consider, for a moment, what you would spend on a survey to check that the structure of your new home is sound. More and more new home owners are engaging the services of Feng Shui consultants and interior designers and giving careful thought to the kinds of materials that they bring into their home. It is logical, therefore, to contact a professional dowser to locate any possible sources of geopathic stress within your new home and get advice on how to eliminate it. You can test drive a car, find a new job with a get-out clause after three months, live with the new love of your life for a month or two before you make a commitment but when it comes to buying a home, it is not so easy to assess whether it is going to work for you.

The earth vibrates with an electromagnetic frequency of about 7.83 Hz which is almost identical to the range of human alpha brainwaves. The physicist W.O. Schumann made this discovery in 1952 and so waves of this frequency are also known as Schumann waves. As an electromagnetic frequency of approximately 7.83 Hz is a vital component of our natural environment, extreme distortions of this level can lead to what is termed geopathic stress. If we are exposed to abnormal frequencies for too long, it can lead to a weakening of the immune system and make us feel exhausted. Other symptoms include mood swings, lethargy, dizziness, irritability and an extreme sensitivity to hot and cold and the weather. It can also cause us to become more mentally active at night leading to insomnia. This, in turn, breaks the cycle of nourishing chi, leaving us feeling tired and ineffective in the mornings.

The US Space Agency, NASA, incorporates imitations of the earth's electromagnetic frequency into their space shuttles. Known as Schumann Resonators, they safe-guard the health of astronauts while they are outside the electromagnetic influence of the earth. The earth naturally creates its own electromagnetic field, but it is when there are underground disturbances in this field that there are potentially harmful effects. Sources of abnormal electromagnetic energy include the presence of under-ground water, underground streams, caverns and man-made sources such as sewers, tunnels and mains electrical supplies. Rich deposits of oil and coal or other minerals can also disturb this field. Two electromagnetic fields have been mapped using two different grid systems. Firstly, the Hartman Net detects a grid which covers the earth along north/south east/west axes (following the lines of longitude and latitude). The other field can be detected through what is known as the 'Curry Grid', in which the magnetic fields are spread out in north-easterly, south-westerly directions. These two grids are diagonally opposite each other, but where they intercept, there is evidence of a very strong geopathic disturbance.

There are a number of ways in which you could detect these harmful rays or 'black streams' within your home. You could either employ a professional to do the detect-ing for you, or you could try dowsing for them yourself. Dowsing is the most popu-lar method of detecting these negative rays and a dowser may use rods, a pendulum, muscle testing or even intuition. It is important to remember that these rays are much stronger at night and that individually they are not a problem. At the points where they intercept, however, they become much stronger. It is vital to make sure that you are not sleeping on an intersection of one of these grids or that you not being affect-ed by them when sitting at your desk or in your favourite chair. (Refer to the Resource Section under 'Dowsing' for further reading and professional help).

Putting aluminium tin foil, cork, cardboard or plastic sheeting under your mattress to deflect these harmful rays provides a short-term solution. But it is far more effec-tive to divert the rays using strategically placed crystals, copper rods or iron rods. Alternatively, you could use the excellent RadiTech device already mentioned to help neutralise and eliminate geopathic stress within the home. This device is plugged into the mains it where quietly gets on with its job. I also recommend read-ing Rolph Gordon's book *Are You Sleeping in a Safe Place?*.

EARTH ACUPUNCTURE

WHILE GEOPATHIC stress may be a modern term for understanding harmful chi emanating from within the earth, traditional Feng Shui masters have understood for centuries how chi is disturbed. Knowledge of mysterious underground energies combined with the ability to dowse their precise location is as integral to Chinese Feng Shui as it is to any other geomantic tradition in the world. All share the same aim – which is to seek healthy chi and to avoid unhealthy Sha Chi.

The Ming Dynasty text, *The Eight Needles of the Water Compass Method*, takes a similar view to that of modern geopathic stress experts. This is that unhealthy chi rises from within the earth as a result of underground veins or Black Streams or meridians that are blocked, stagnant or unhealthy. These Black Streams are seen as particularly dangerous when they converge or cross one another, even if the vertical distance between them is great. There is also a link between earth meridians that are traumatised and the effect that this has on the landscape above. Typical sources of this trauma include railway, motorway and tunnel construction, excavations for cuttings and embankments, and mines and quarrying. Disturbance of these vital meridians can also be caused by building foundations – especially those with steel footings or deep basements. Other disturbances come from power stations, electricity sub-stations, military bases, steel pilings, telegraph poles and even road traffic signs. On an even more vibrational level, Sha Chi can be retained from human trauma and suffering on a site. This can include battles, witch burnings and executions. Finally, on an even more subtle level, constructing a home, hospital, airport, public building or housing estate without any form of traditional foundation stone laying ceremony can also cause disturbance. This is because the construction and disturbance of the earth without making offerings in good faith to the nature spirits whose land has been taken is considered to be a source of trauma and therefore of Sha Chi.

In Chinese texts paths of concentrated energy were symbolised by the dragon.

Earth acupuncture is a powerful remedy designed to cure unhealthy Sha Chi and transform it into healthy Sheng Chi. Earth acupuncture utilises different 'needles' which include metal rods, wooden stakes, stones and crystals. These are either driven into the ground or placed on the surface at the appropriate earth acupuncture points for a specified time. The 'treatment' can range from a few seconds to two hours. With a large meridian or with a major geological fault, the 'needle' may need to be left in place permanently. Fire, in the form of candles, incense or a bonfire can also be employed. Other permanent needles may take the form of moving water features, sculptures, standing stones or an auspiciously planted tree. (For more details on earth acupuncture see Resource Guide).

PART · FIVE

INTEGRATION

Chapter Twelve

Integrating the Components of Feng Shui

YOU NOW HAVE THE OPPORTUNITY to sift through the information so far and decide what you need to deal with next on your Feng Shui journey. In this section, I will take you through a step-by-step approach to the subject that we have covered so far which will enable you to:

1. Begin to put in place the changes you need on your current journey

2. Use these components again in the future to review your situation when you are at a turning point. This could involve: moving home, changing job, beginning a new relationship, a change of season or when you feel your chi is low or stagnant.

WHO YOU ARE

FROM THE MATERIAL in Chapter 3, you will have gained an insight into your unique horoscope based on 9-Star Ki Astrology. From this new perspective, it is possible to see where your creative strengths lie and whether you are currently exploring these or not. Which element is your Principal Number – is this element reflected in your current living environment? How can you enhance your element within your space using the various tools in Chapter 2 and the fine tuning from Chapter 9.

How do you relate to others in your life at present? Take a look at the table in

Chapter 4 on page 71 in which you have drawn up your horoscope alongside those of members of your family, your partner, children, and colleagues. How do you relate to them? Where are the potential antagonisms? Even if it looks to be a challenging combination on paper, knowing who you are and respecting who they are can help you form a more understanding relationship.

WHERE YOU ARE

FROM THE TABLES and information in Chapter 4, it is now possible to predict which House you occupy in any given year. Alongside this material you can see what is potentially in store for you at that time. Are you working with the tide at present or are you going against it? When planning my year's activities I have always found it useful to maintain an overall sense of what I would like to achieve. I always use this formula to help in this decision-making process as I have found on reflection that working with the House that I occupy, rather than against it, makes for greater success.

For example, if you are occupying the 4 House – movement without stability – then you need to be aware that it is easy to become overenthusiastic, making too many commitments for example, with the result that you could fail to live up to your promises. On the other hand, you could use this new found rising surge of chi energy to continue, extend or expand on what you have already begun to develop in the previous year (3 House). Each House has its potentials and its pitfalls.

DIRECTIONS

FROM CHAPTER 5, you will have worked out which directions to be careful of, or avoid, at any given time. In the same way that a navigator would take into account the state of the tides, currents and wind, knowing how the chi is currently flowing relative to you in any given year can help to make moves that go with the flow rather than against it. Look back at your own life when you have made major moves, recall the direction that was involved and see whether the move was successful or difficult.

HEALTH

LEVELS OF CHI ARE in a constant state of flux reflecting your stamina, appetite and overall well-being. These fluctuating levels of chi are not as predictable as the astrological fluctuations that can be discovered using 9-Star Ki Astrology. Since you yourself are such a vital component in the practice and implementation of successful Feng Shui, it is important to assess the current state of your chi. From the information in Chapter 5, you can begin to unravel some of the fascinating material that has evolved over the centuries from Oriental Diagnosis. Again, you can use this self-assessment programme time and time again to review your needs on your future journey.

In Chapter 6, I have shown that there are many paths you can take to re-balance your chi over a 10–30 day period. This section not only explains how to bring about inner change but also how to implement change within the home using Feng Shui. Remember that any Feng Shui remedies that you put into place relative to your current health will need to be reviewed from time to time. Feng Shui identifies your strengths as well as your weaknesses and makes your journey that much smoother.

The main thing to remember about your health is that you see the world through your current condition. If, for example, you identify that your current health reveals a depletion of Metal energy – acute stagnation connected with the lungs or large intestine – then your 'outlook' will be gloomy, despondent, uncommunicative, dark and pessimistic. This in, turn, will naturally make your chi feel more at home in a similar sort of environment, somewhere dark, isolated and cold. Following the same lines, you will also be attracted to foods, activities and forms of lifestyle that also reflect a more Metal imbalance, such as foods that over cooked or re-heated, a solitary existence or intellectual activity. In this case the answer lies in bringing more of the positive attributes of the Metal element into place using Feng Shui, and by supporting this element with its predecessor element, Soil/Earth.

FENG SHUI

ALWAYS BEGIN BY taking care of the 'big picture' – the form, the landscape, the layout and the chi of your immediate environment. This is fundamental to whatever approach or school of Feng Shui you may draw inspiration from. It is like constructing the foundations of a building, or tilling the land before you plant. Take care of the obvious – deflect any negative chi and arrange the layout of your rooms from a practical Feng Shui perspective, as outlined in Chapter 8.

There are so many different styles and layers to traditional Feng Shui that in Chapter 10 I have chosen to share with you one of the fundamental approaches to Compass School Feng Shui that is simple to understand and apply. By identifying which of the eight life aspirations you need or wish to enhance at present, you can utilise the tools that are mentioned in both Chapters 2 and 10 to bring about these changes. Again, like your health and your astrology, do review this from time to time. While it might seem appropriate right now to work on your career, for example, in six months' time you may feel out of touch with your family and need to work on that particular mansion or sector within your home.

I learnt something quite early in my Feng Shui practice which I must share with you. I soon discovered that Feng Shui was far more effective if I enhanced not only the relevant life aspiration sector of my room or home but also took care of this sector in my work area. Whether this is a desk, office or clinic, be aware that this mansion also reflects what your aspirations at home should be and must be kept well clear of any clutter, baggage or stagnation. It is also advisable to take a compass with you when you are staying in a hotel or a friend's home for the weekend. Being aware of your space and making minor adjustments to your sleeping environment can make all the difference. Remember, you are like a living, walking Pakua yourself!

INTENTION

EFFECTIVE USE OF FENG SHUI depends on the strength and quality of the intention that you put into the job. In many traditional practices of Feng Shui remedies were always accompanied by some form of ritual. Whether space clearing was practised first, using chanting, symbols, gongs or incense, or whether a declaration or prayer was chanted, undoubtedly the power of the remedies was enhanced by the intention behind them. The time of day is also important. Chi is at its most active between the hours of 7 am and 1 pm, for example. Casually moving a piece of furniture, hanging a new painting, placing a wind chime while thinking about supper, or even wondering whether anything is going to happen, is likely to negate a possible successful outcome. Instead, make your changes with an uncluttered mind, no distractions and clear intention, .

On a subliminal level, the remedies that we use in Feng Shui can also act as a reminder of your intention. Every time you see that crystal, plant, or the new position of your bed, you are unconsciously reminded of what it is you are trying to achieve on your journey. It is easy to understand that once you make your intention or declaration clear, the journey and the changes start to fall into line.

FURTHER STUDY

FENG SHUI IS undoubtedly a fascinating subject and one that we can all benefit from. Like any traditional wisdom, there are many different paths to choose from. The information I have put together in this book is primarily based on what I have discovered works for me, together with what I have found as a practitioner to be accessible and practical to other people. What you have before you is an opening into this cornucopia of study and practice. There are many more layers to Feng Shui that I could not begin to share with you in a book of this size. The astrological components of Feng Shui comprise a massive study that would take years of patient and precise application to fully comprehend. If you are drawn to this aspect of Feng Shui, please refer to the Further Reading Section in the Resource Section at the back of this book.

If you are hungry to learn more, then in addition to reading the books in the Resource Section, why not attend an introductory lecture or seminar, or enrol in one of the schools that offer professional training in Feng Shui? Not only is it a fascinating journey but your companions will share with your desire and commitment to learn more. Try to be open to what you hear or read, there are many different approaches and perspectives being put forward and they all have value. For me, Feng Shui is about creating health, luck and prosperity which can be summed up in one word, 'freedom'. There is little freedom in being critical, dogmatic, rigid, secular or intolerant! Freedom is far more about being flexible and adaptable in a changing world – the essence of how we are successful in any journey in life.

LESS IS MORE

WHEN WE TAKE ON any new subject there is a temptation to get completely carried away with it. In our excitement and thrill, we want to Feng Shui every square inch of our own space and everybody else's! I was very much like this in my early days but, on reflection, now appreciate that a few well intentioned appropriate changes are far more meaningful than 30 or 40 hastily made adjustments. Allow 10–30 days for the changes to begin to take effect. It is very tempting to work on every sector of your home – indeed you may feel that you are not doing the job correctly unless you have utilised every single remedy in the book! In any subject you name, a professional can troubleshoot a problem and bring about effective change simply and efficiently without causing undue chaos. But it takes years and years of experience, intuition and skill to make this possible. Feng Shui is much the same. With constantly fiddling and tweaking, it is not possible to see the wood for the trees. Be patient, curious and try to keep it all simple and practical. If you can just find that one trigger that will pop all the other disjointed pieces into place, then Eureka! You have discovered Feng Shui!

BON VOYAGE

I WISH YOU EVERY success on your journey through life and I know that this book can form a very valuable part of your travel kit. Use the information in much the same way that you would use a compass. Refer to it from time to time, let it back up and substantiate your journey, your will and your dream. I have always found Feng Shui to be a most effective way of turning my dream and my intuition into physical reality. Living as we do in a changing world, it is important to get a bearing on who and where we are, and appreciate that our inner and outer worlds are interconnected. This seemingly ageless and timeless that wisdom has come to us from China may seem alien in this day and age, but I can assure you that, within the next 30 years, it will become mainstream. It will not just be the concept and practice of Feng Shui that will become more readily accepted, but also a fundamental understanding that all phenomena are interconnected. For too long we have lived in a world of segregation and division that has created an introspective and short-sighted view of ourselves, our environment and our future. I hope that your experience of Feng Shui will enhance your vision and faith in the future that lies ahead.

Glossary

Bagua	*see* Pakua
Cardinal points	North, south, east and west
Chi (or Ki)	'Cosmic breath' – the motivating life force or energy
Compass School	School of Feng Shui which utilises the Lo P'an compass
Cutting Chi	*see* Secret Arrows
Feng	Wind
Feng Sha	Poisonous wind
Feng Shui Shien-Sheng	A Feng Shui Master
Five Elements	Water, Fire, Earth, Metal and Wood
Form School	Use of the landscape to assess auspicious chi flow
Hexagram	A symbol made up of eight broken or unbroken lines formed from two trigrams. There are 64 different hexagrams.
I Ching	*The Book of Changes* – the Chinese classic based on the 64 hexagrams
Intercardinal points	South-west, south-east, north-west, north-east
Ki	*see* chi
Kua	I trigram

Life aspirations	Representations of the compass directions of the Pakua
Lo P'An/Luo P'An	Feng Shui compass
Lo Shu	Taoist Magic Square with nine Houses associated with the Later Heaven arrangement of trigrams
Lung	Dragon
Lung Mei	Dragon meridians or veins
Magic Square	*see* Lo Shu
Pakua	An eight-sided or circular arrangement of eight trigrams
Poison Arrow	*see* Secret Arrow
Secret Arrow	A potentially destructive influence of negative chi
Sha Chi	Unfavourable, harmful chi
Shen	Spirits
Sheng Chi	Healthy chi
Shui	Water
Taoism	Chinese belief in the Tao – 'The Way' concerned with harmony and flow
Trigram (or Kua)	A symbol made up of three horizontal lines, broken or unbroken, respectively (also known as Kua) representing yin or yang. There are eight in total. Two trigrams form the basis of a Hexagram.
Yang	Active or activating energy
Yin	Passive or sedentary energy

Resources

BOOKS

FENG SHUI

Simon Brown, *Practical Feng Shui*, Ward Lock, 1997

Lam Kam Chuen, *The Feng Shui Handbook*, Gaia Books, 1996

E. J. Itel, *Feng Shui*, Graham Brash, 1995

Man-Ho Kwok, Joanne O'Brien, *The Elements of Feng Shui*, Element Books, 1996

Man-Ho Kwok, Joanne O'Brien, *The Feng Shui Kit*, Piatkus, 1995

Gina Lazenby, *The Feng Shui House Book*, Conran Octopus, 1998

Jami Lin, *Contemporary Earth Design*, Earth Design, 1997

Evelyn Lipp, *Chinese Geomancy*, Times Books International, 1979

Sara Rossbach, *Feng Shui*, Rider, 1988

Sara Rossbach, *Interior Design with Feng Shui*, Century Publishing, 1988

Raphael Simons, *Feng Shui Step by Step*, Rider, 1996

Stephen Skinner, *The Living Earth Manual of Feng Shui*, Penguin Books, 1996

Stephen Skinner, *Feng Shui 1999*, Parragon, 1998

William Spear, *Feng Shui Made Easy*, Thorsons, 1995

Sarah Surety, *Feng Shui for Your Home*, Rider, 1997

Lilian Too, *The Complete Illustrated Guide to Feng Shui*, Element

Lilian Too, *Essential Feng Shui*, Rider, 1998

Derek Walters, *The Feng Shui Handbook*, Aquarian Press 1991

Eva Wong, *Feng Shui*, Shambala Publications, 1996

SPACE CLEARING
Karen Kingston, *Creating Sacred Space with Feng Shui*, Piatkus, 1996
Denise Linn, *Sacred Space*, Rider, 1995

CLUTTER
Karen Kingston, *Clear Your Clutter with Feng Shui*, Piatkus, 1998
Declan Treacy, *Clear Your Desk*, Century Business, 1992

GARDENING
Gill Hale, *The Feng Shui Garden*, Aurum Press, 1998

ARCHITECTURE AND INTERIOR DESIGN
T. Mann, *Sacred Architecture*, Element Books, 1993
David Pearson, *The Natural House Book*, Conran Octopus, 1992

GEOPATHIC ENERGY AND RADIATION
David Cowan, Rodney Girdlestone, *Safe as Houses*, Gateway Books, 1996
Rolf Gordon, *Are You Sleeping in a Safe Place?* The Dulwich Health Society,
   130 Gypsy Hill, London SE19 1PL
Jane Thurnell-Read, *Geopathic Stress*, Element Books, 1995

GEOMANCY
Peter Dawkins, *Zoence*, Wigmore Publications, 1995
Martin Palmer, Nigel Palmer, *Sacred Britain*, Piatkus, 1997

DOWSING
Sig Lonegren, *Sig Lonegren's Dowsing Rod Kit*, Virgin Books, 1995

HEALTHY HOMES
Jane Alexander, *Spirit of the Home*, Thorsons, 1998
Susie Chiazzari, *The Healing Home*, Rider, 1998
Dennis Fairchild, *Healing Homes*, Wave Field Publication, 1996

NINE-STAR KI ASTROLOGY
Takashi Yoshikawa, *The Ki*, Rider, 1998
Michio Kushi, *Nine-Star Ki*, One Peaceful Press, 1995
Rex Lassalle, *Grasshopping*, Lassalle, 1998
Bob Sachs, *The Complete Guide to 9-Star Ki*, Element Books, 1992

Jon Sandifer, *Feng Shui Astrology*, Piatkus, 1997
Gerry Thompson, *Feng Shui Astrology for Lovers*, Thorsons, 1998

NINE-STAR KI ALMANAC
9 Ki Resources, P.O. Box 638, Great Barrington, MA 01230-0638, USA

ORIENTAL HEALING
Ted Kaptchuk, *Chinese Medicine*, Rider, 1983
Michio Kushi, *Holistic Health*, Japan Publication, 1993
Jon Sandifer, *Acupressure*, Element, 1997
Jon Sandifer, *The 10 Day Re-Balance Programme*, Rider, 1998

SHOPS AND MAIL ORDER SERVICES

Denise Linn, P. O. Box 75657, Seattle, WA 98125-0657 USA
Esoterica, 5a Devonshire Road, London W4 2EU UK
The Feng Shui Catalogue, Green Dragon House, 16 Goldsmith Road, London W3 6PX UK
The Feng Shui Company, 37 Ballard House, Norway Street, London SE10 9DD UK
Feng Shui Warehouse, P. O. Box 3005, San Diego, CA 2163-1005 USA
The Geomancer, P. O. Box 250, Woking, Surrey GU21 1YY UK

EARTH ACUPUNCTURE

Landscope, Beech View, Crowborough Road, Nutley, East Sussex TN22 3HY UK

ELECTROMAGNETIC STRESS DETECTORS AND ELIMINATORS

Coghill Research Laboratories, Lower Race, Pontypool, Gwent NP4 5UF

GEOPATHIC STRESS ELIMINATORS

Jan Cisek, 8 The Warwick, 68 Richmond Hill, Richmond, Surrey TW10 6RH UK
Dulwich Health Society, 130 Gypsy Hill, London SE19 1PL UK
The Fortunate Blessings Foundation, 24 Village Green Drive, Litchfield, CT 06759, USA

MAGAZINES

Feng Shui for Modern Living, 1 – 5 Clerkenwell Road, London EC1M 5PA UK
Feng Shui Journal, P. O. Box 3005, San Diego, CA 92163-3005 USA
Feng Shui Guild, P. O. Box 766, Boulder, CO 80306 USA

WEBSITES

Chinese Feng Shui Services International: http://www.fengshui.uk.com
Feng Shui Emporium: http://www.luckycat.com
Feng Shui for Modern Living: http://www.fengshui-magazine.com
Feng Shui Network International: http://www.fengshuinet.com
Feng Shui Society Home Page: http://www.fengshuisociety.org.uk
The Geomancer: http://www.dragonmagic.com
Roger Green: http://www.real.net.au./~fengshui
Karen Kingston: http://www.spaceclearing.com
Denise Linn: http://www.qed-productions.com
Jon Sandifer: http://www.jonsandifer.com
William Spear: http://membersaol.com/fengshuime/wmhtml
Lilian Too: http://www.lilian-too.com

NON-PROFIT-MAKING ORGANISATIONS

The Feng Shui Society, 377 Edgware Road, London W2 1BT, U.K.
Tel: 07050 289200
e.mail: karenayers@fengshuisociety.org.uk
Website: http://ww.fengshuisociety.org.uk
International Feng Shui Society, 58 Tristania Street, Loganholme 4129, Queensland, Australia
e.mail: lccc@ozemail.com.au
Fax: ++ 61 738013217

STUDYING FENG SHUI

Naturally, there are many different routes that you could pursue to further your interest in Feng Shui. This could involve reading more, attending a lecture, having a consultation in your own home, attending an international conference, enrolling in a weekend course or finding a school which offers professional training.

If you would like to become a professional Feng Shui consultant, I would advise you to write to any of the schools listed in *Feng Shui for Modern Living* or contact the Feng Shui Society in the UK or the International Feng Shui Society in Australia for a list of schools that you could approach.

It is important to remember that, at the present time (1999), there are no currently recognised standards, regulations or certification procedures in place. It is therefore vital that you approach any of the schools as an individual and check out what they have to offer, who their teachers are, and what support and follow up you will receive as you train. As with any subject, the best way to study is to do the ground work, put in the hours and apply yourself as well as you possibly can. It could take several years of study before you are competent at Feng Shui and at handling the client/consultant relationship. Even then, there is always more to learn. Feng Shui is a lifetime study and the knowledge you acquire needs to be assimilated. Naturally, it takes time for us all to mature and develop as a consultant.

THE FENG SHUI SOCIETY (UK)

The Feng Shui Society was established in 1993 as an unincorporated, non-profit making association to advance Feng Shui principles and concepts as a contribution to the creation of harmonious environments for individuals and society in general. The Society serves as a focus for the exchange of information and experience, both of the professional Feng Shui community and for others wishing to develop their knowledge and apply the principles in their own lives. The Feng Shui Society offers members:

- A programme of Society events throughout the country

- Discussion groups and case studies

- A monthly newsletter with articles and book reviews

- A book, video and tape library

- An information pack with details of books, courses, shops, Feng Shui consultants and an excellent introduction to the different styles and approaches to Feng Shui

REGISTERED CONSULTANTS OF THE FENG SHUI SOCIETY

In 1997 the Society appealed to its professional members to consider forming a professional body that could initially set up a code of ethics for Feng Shui practitioners and later develop educational standards that would provide a minimum background and training for anyone setting up as a Feng Shui consultant. The current members of the register of consultants of the Feng Shui Society helped to draft, agree and sign a voluntary code of ethics in 1997. This was a first and major step in bringing together Feng Shui consultants. In 1998 the Society put a two-year time frame in place towards establishing the educational standards that the various Feng Shui schools, consultants and teachers could agree would be the future benchmark for determining the educational status of a Feng Shui consultant. It is a big challenge, given the many different styles and approaches to Feng Shui, but at least the dialogue has begun and there is growing interest in the United States and Australia in what the Society has initiated.

WORKSHOPS AND CONSULTATIONS WITH JON SANDIFER

For details of my consultation services, my teaching schedule worldwide or my other books, please contact me at:

Jon Sandifer
P.O. Box 69
Teddington
Middlesex TW11 9SH
United Kingdom

Tel/Fax: 0181-977 8988
e.mail: jon_sandifer@compuserve.com
website: http://www.jonsandifer.com

Index